ISSUE 1:2 → KIKU **ADATTO** · DAVID **BRESKIN** · JO ANN **CALLIS** · WILLIAM **CHRISTENBERRY** · JAMES **CRUMP** · JEANNE **DUNNING** · MERRY **FORESTA** · RICK **HOCK** · DAVID **LEVINTHAL** · MICHAEL **LIGHT** · MARTHA **MADIGAN** · ANN **MANDELBAUM** · DAN **MEINWALD** · SUZANNE **OPTON** · GAY **OUTLAW** · RENNY **PRITIKIN** · C.P. **ROSENTHAL** · FAZAL **SHEIKH** · ELLIOT **SCHWARTZ** · KENNETH **SHORR** · VALERIE **SOE** · JANICE **TANNIN** · CARLA **WILLIAMS**

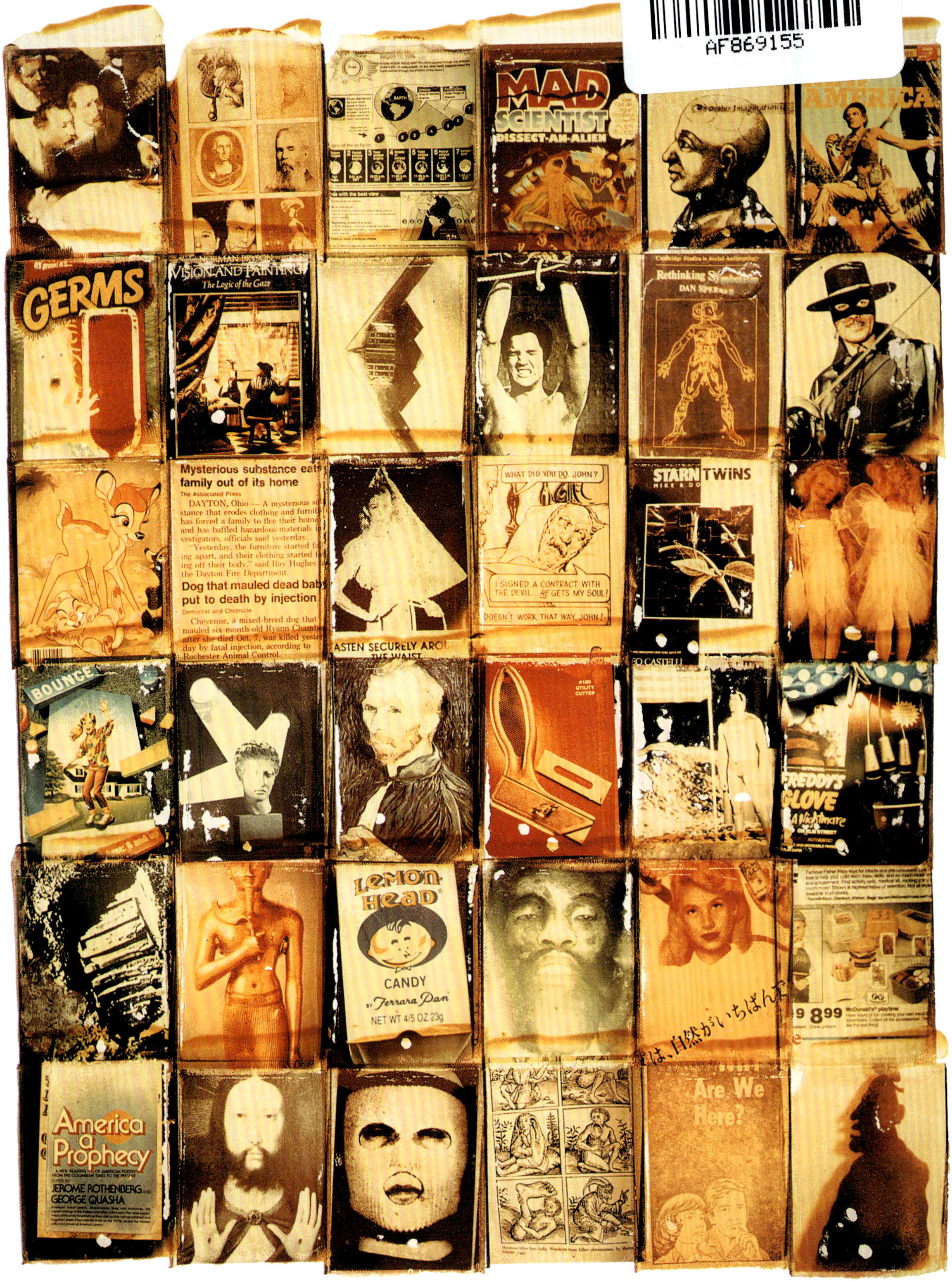

Cover: Janice Tannin, Untitled, 1991. This page: Rick Hock, *Codex: America, a Prophecy*, 1989.

The Friends of Photography, San Francisco

Join The Friends of Photography

Members enjoy benefits including: see, a quarterly journal of visual culture • Collector Print Program • Limited Editions Program • Free admission to the Ansel Adams Center for Photography • Discounts at The Friends of Photography Bookstore • Workshops, lectures and gallery talks • Children's and school programs • Awards to artists • Connections Network • Portfolio reviews

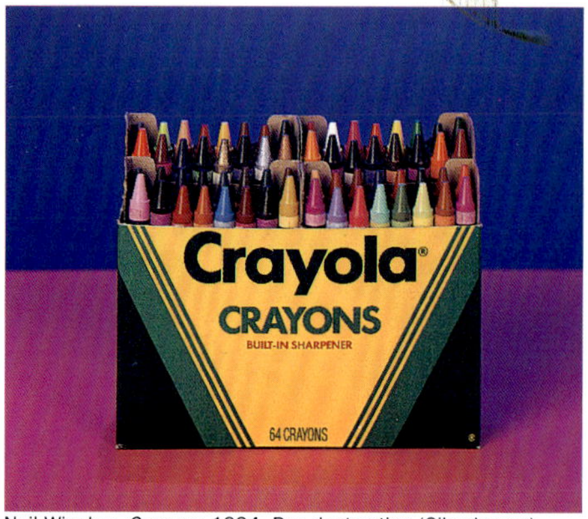

Neil Winokur, *Crayons*, 1994. Dye destruction (Cibachrome) print, 10 1/2 by 13 1/2 inch image on 11 by 14 inch paper. Courtesy of the artist and Janet Borden Inc., New York

Collector Print Program

See the future of the image

For information about membership and the Collector Print Program, contact:
The Friends of Photography
250 Fourth Street
San Francisco CA 94103
Phone 415.495.7000
Fax 415.495.8517
E-mail seeFOP@aol.com

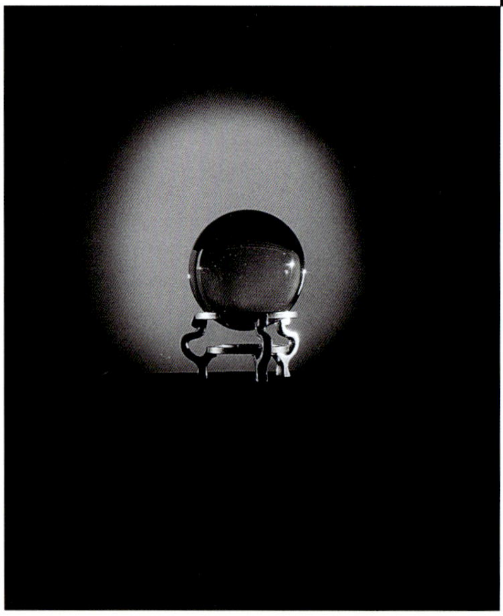

As a benefit of membership in The Friends of Photography, members at the Sustaining level ($300) and above participate in the Collector Print Program, an easy and exciting way to start or add to your own collection of original, signed photographs. Each year, the program offers a diverse selection of photographic styles and artists, both well known and emerging. Prints in the program are available exclusively through The Friends of Photography.

1995 Collector Print Program: Marion Brenner, William Heick, Kate Jordahl, Wright Morris, J. John Priola, Cindy Sherman, Neil Winokur

J. John Priola, *Crystal Ball*, 1994. Gelatin silver print, 16 3/4 by 13 3/4 inch image on 16 3/4 by 13 3/4 inch paper. Courtesy of the artist, Fraenkel Gallery, San Francisco and Paul Kopeikin Gallery, Los Angeles

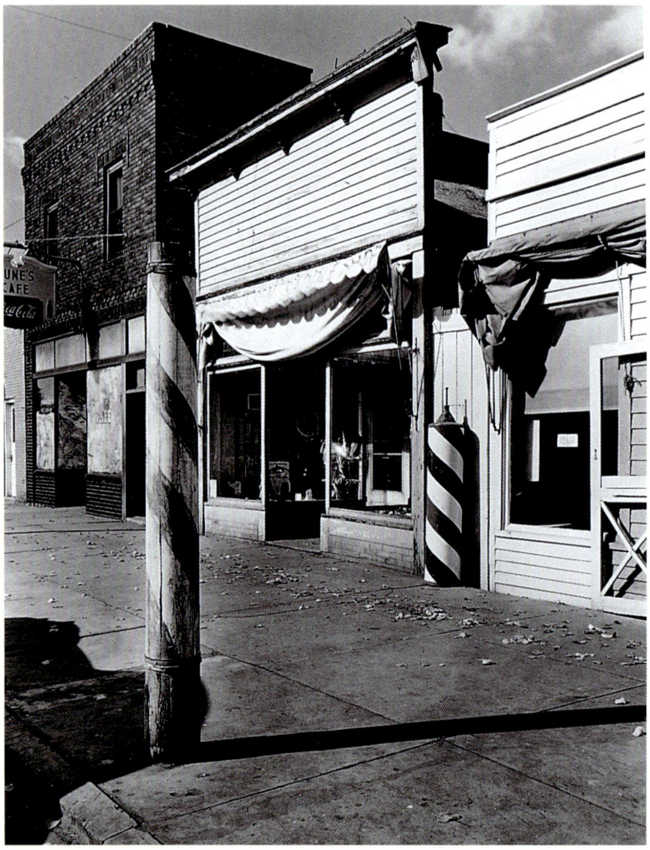

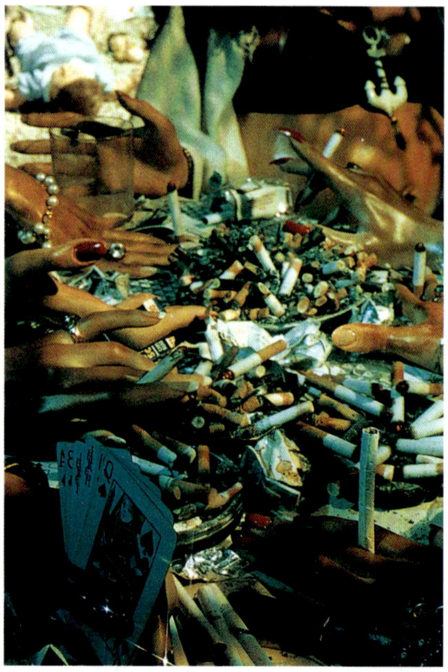

Cindy Sherman, Untitled, 1988, printed 1994. Chromogenic print, 13 1/2 by 10 1/2 inch image on 14 by 11 inch paper. Courtesy of the artist and Metro Pictures, New York

Left: Wright Morris, *Central City, Nebraska*, 1948, printed 1994. Gelatin silver print, 12 1/2 by 9 1/2 inch image on 14 by 11 inch paper. Courtesy of the artist.

see: a journal of visual culture

Editor in Chief
Andy Grundberg

Editor
Michael Read

Associate Editor
Steven Jenkins

Design
Toki Design

Editorial Assistants
Holly Erickson
Gustavus Kundahl
Charlene Rule

Advertising Coordinator
Charlene Rule

Issue 1:2/ 1995

ISSN 1076-4550, ISBN 0-262-56088-7

see is published by The Friends of Photography

see also is distributed worldwide by MIT Press, Cambridge, Massachusetts and London, England.

The publication of see is made possible with the support of the Andy Warhol Foundation for the Visual Arts, the California Arts Council, Grants for the Arts of the City of San Francisco, and the members of The Friends of Photography.

Second class postage paid at San Francisco, CA, and additional mailing offices. Printed in Hong Kong by C & C Offset Printing Co., Ltd.

Editorial and advertising address:
250 Fourth Street
San Francisco CA 94103
phone: 415.495.7000
fax: 415.495.8517
E-mail: SEEfop@aol.com

CONTENTS

The Friends of Photography

While the objectivity and veracity of photographic information recently has been challenged by both theory and practice, the power of images to evoke strong emotions never has been at issue in the critical debates of our time. This makes for an unsettling paradox: pictures that are patently unreal and/or ambiguous can still move us to tears, outrage and anger. Andres Serrano's picture"Piss Christ," seized on by the Christian Right as an example of all that is wrong with government funding for the arts, is a classic case: non-art viewers see red in a picture that is, on the face of it, at least, a cheap plastic crucifix in a field of yellow. → William Christenberry and David Levinthal recently have shown work that challenges two other sacred cows: the Ku Klux Klan and the Holocaust. This is loaded territory enough, but their decision to portray their subject matter indirectly, through doll-like figurines, raises the ante. Do they make matters worse by transforming painful histories into innocuous docudramas, in the manner of network television (Woody, Mia, Michael Jackson, O.J. *et al.*, all made less real by being portrayed as fiction), or do they address the territory of the inexpressible by means of a necessary distancing device? → These are questions taken up by the two artists in conversation with Merry Foresta, the Curator of Photography at the Smithsonian's National Museum of American Art and, we're pleased to say, the newest addition to our illustrious Editorial Board. Also welcomed in this issue: Kiku Adatto, our columnist on public images, and new fiction and poetry by C.P. Rosenthal and David Breskin. In addition, with "Sound and Vision" we're reviewing CD-ROM titles for the first time (something we suspect we'll be doing more of in the future) and introducing a section devoted to the history of lens-based images, called "Perspectives." Remember: you see it first in see.
—Andy Grundberg,
Editor-in-Chief

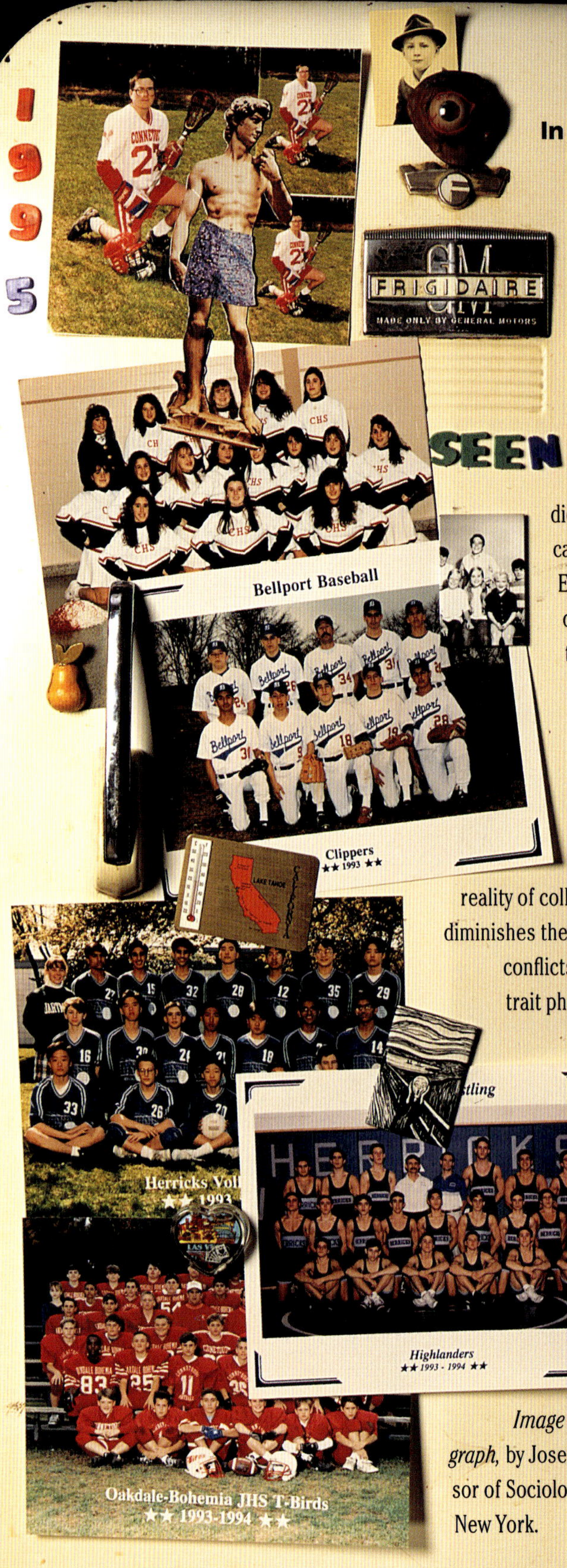

In teams (and in social life generally), there is a dialectic between the group and the individual.... The role of the photographer in organizing the team photograph is fundamentally as an agent of social control.... The formalized "public relations" of the team photograph—designed, planned and organized by social convention and custom—is the opposite of a candid "action shot" in which the camera captures a more spontaneous reality. Except for some unpredictable deviant cases of obscene finger gestures or closed eyes, the photographic control of the image is almost total.... From a postmodern point of view, the team photo is an idealized Disneyland memento of a standardized and ideological experience that not only distorts the reality of collective experience on teams but also diminishes the reality of individual differences and conflicts.... The mass appeal of group portrait photography is also consistent with a postmodern obsession with images. Sociologically, the team photograph diminishes the reality of individual differences and conflicts and certifies an unreal world order of conformity and sameness.

—From the essay *Image and Meaning in the Team Photograph*, by Joseph E. Behar, Ph.D. Behar is a Professor of Sociology at Dowling College in Oakdale, New York.

seen

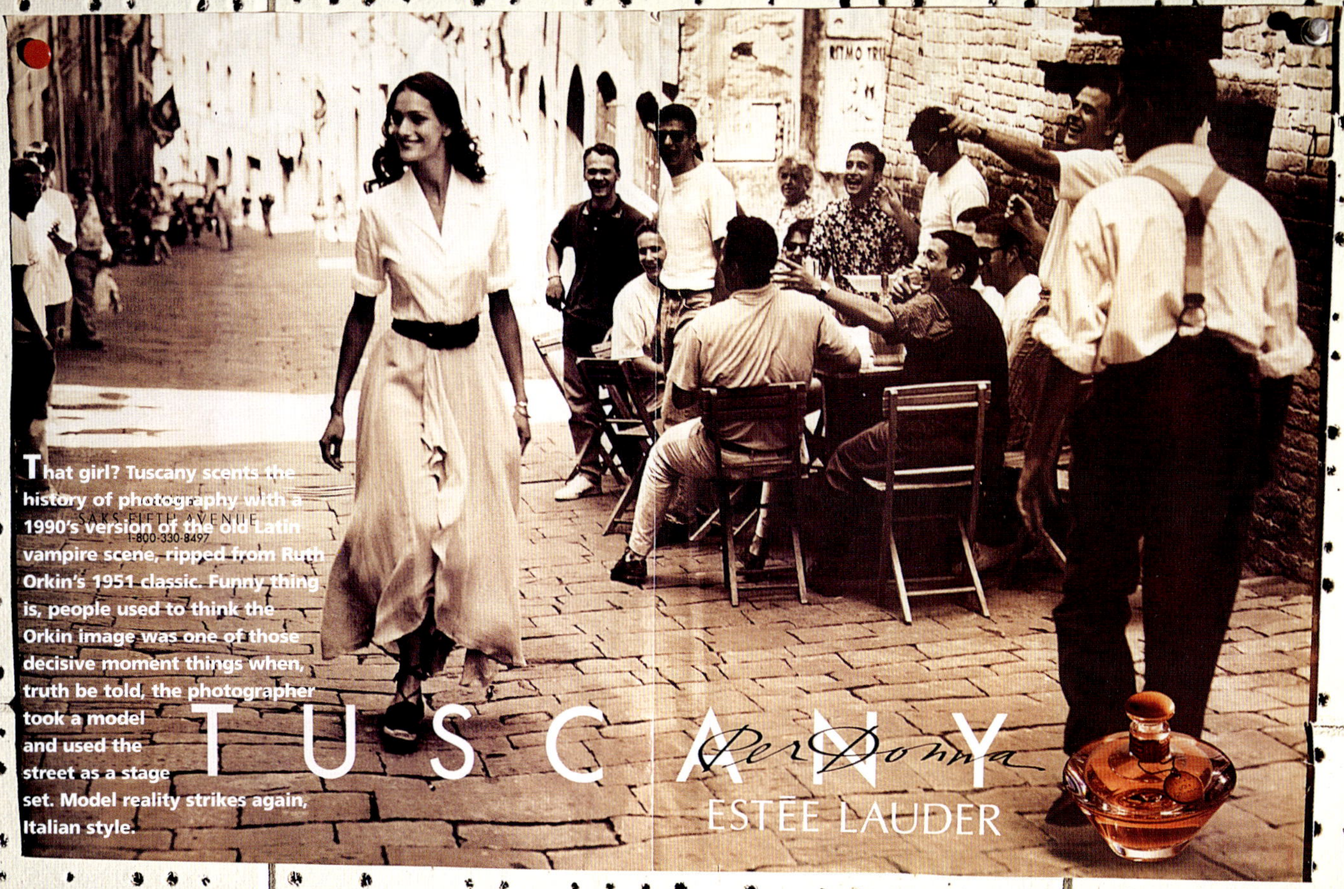

That girl? Tuscany scents the history of photography with a 1990's version of the old Latin vampire scene, ripped from Ruth Orkin's 1951 classic. Funny thing is, people used to think the Orkin image was one of those decisive moment things when, truth be told, the photographer took a model and used the street as a stage set. Model reality strikes again, Italian style.

Media Watch

Some things I know about Jo

Jo falls into things. As a fledgling photographer, she showed her portfolio of sensitive, black-and-white prints to the advertising agency where Allison (her next-door neighbor) and Amanda (her landlord) work, and before you could say "snapshot" she was on assignment for a major maker of men's underwear.

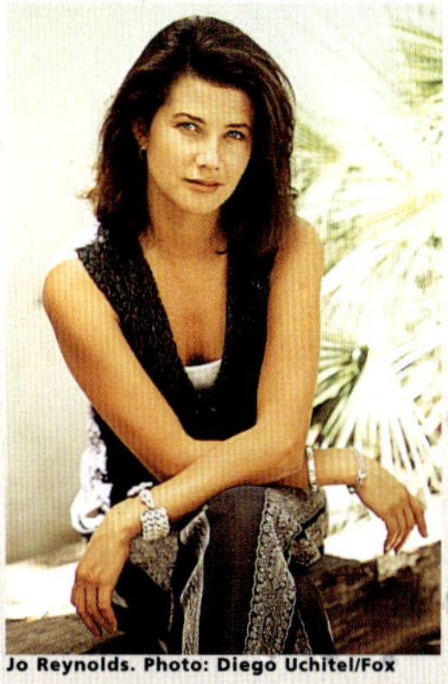
Jo Reynolds. Photo: Diego Uchitel/Fox

Jo screws up. Jo blew the assignment (at least according to Amanda) because she had the model strip off his underpants and pose totally buff. Jo felt she'd done something creative, but Amanda was livid. Later, Jo falls in love with Reed, an ex-con. Then she kills him. Then she finds out he's the father of her unborn child.

Jo lucks out. Jo discovers a beautiful young model, Sarah, who is going to be the next big thing in the fashion world. Jo photographs her on the back of the very boat on which she killed Reed but that now belongs to Jake, Amanda's new boyfriend and Jo's boyfriend before the ex-con (but stay tuned). Jo lets Sarah stay with her in her second-story Melrose Place apartment, but the model's ex-boyfriend follows in pursuit and pushes Jo down the stairs.

Jo's full name is Jo Beth Reynolds. She's played by an actress named Daphne Zuniga.

Jo's big new discovery, Sarah, takes a powder from *Melrose Place* and ends up on *Models, Inc.*, a total drag of a show until (trumpets please) Reed shows up again, undead. Jo, given a summer to recover from the push down the stairs, carries her baby to full term.

Jo uses a Yashica FR, with a normal lens and a flash in the hotshoe. At least that's what she carries in the publicity shots supplied by Spelling Entertainment, which created *Melrose Place.* Jo also carries her own gear, such as it is. She doesn't use strobes or reflectors. She's a fashion photographer lite.

Jo feeds into everyone's notion of being a photographer. It's like being a poet: scribe a few sensitive, interior-dialogue type lines and you are one. The distance between you and creative accomplishment is narrowed, if not erased, in your own mind. Jo's pictures, no matter how trite and banal (and the few we're allowed to see certainly are that), reflect her enormous sensitivity to the visual world. She's a kind of weeping eyeball, a ready repository for all the sorry sights she has witnessed from her Melrose Place apartment.

Saintly as she is, Jo is sexy in an earthy kind of way. She's humus to everyone else's desires—especially Jake's, although he's supposed to be smitten by Amanda. Photography is a sign of Jo's fertility; its penchant for filling the frame with the world, and the world with images, produces the same kind of emotional overcharge as Jo's penchant for picking the wrong guys.

Jo is a mixed bag. She gives birth to a beautiful baby but is unlucky enough to have it in the hospital where her friends Michael and Kimberly are residents. Well, I don't have to tell you about Michael and Kimberly. Or Sidney, for that matter. It gets worse. Much worse.
—Andy Grundberg

Next on Melrose Place: *Jo's photographs are digitized and sent out on the Internet without copyright protection!*

perspectives

COMPILED BY DEBORAH KLOCHKO

The idea for the camera existed two thousand years before photography was invented. A snail taught the ancient Greeks and Romans about light-sensitive emulsions. The Chinese invented eyeglasses three hundred years before they first appeared in Europe. A person's character was determined by the bumps on his or her head.

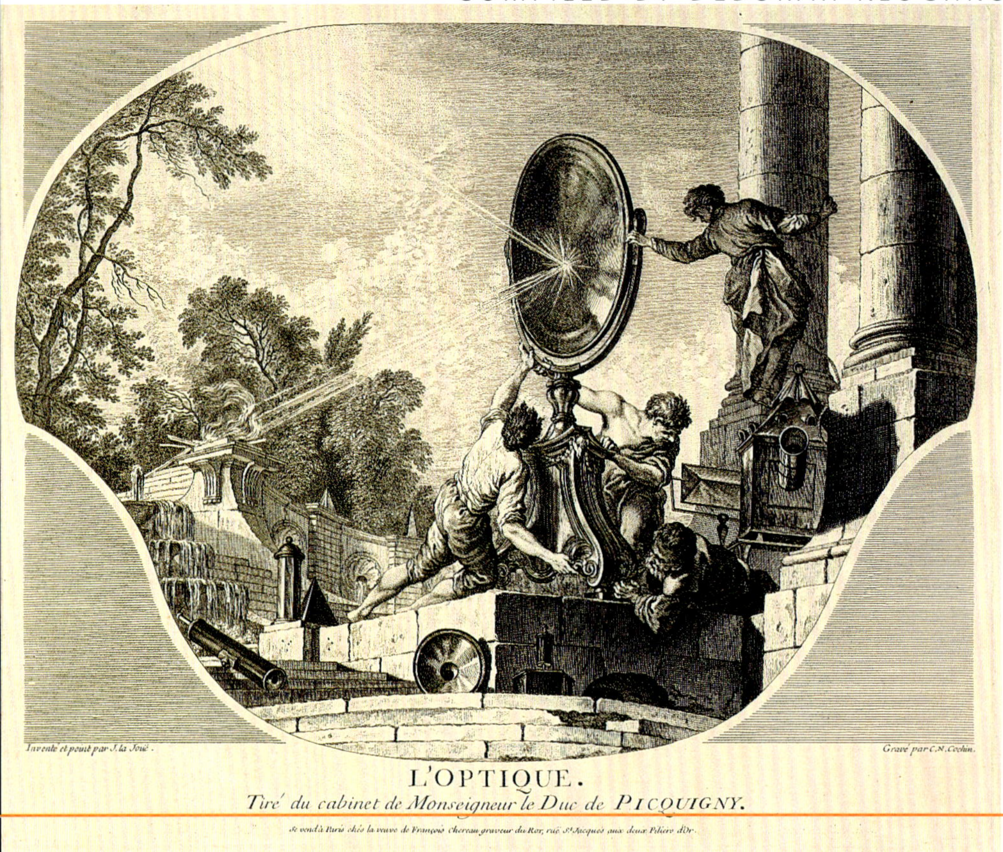

Art & Invention

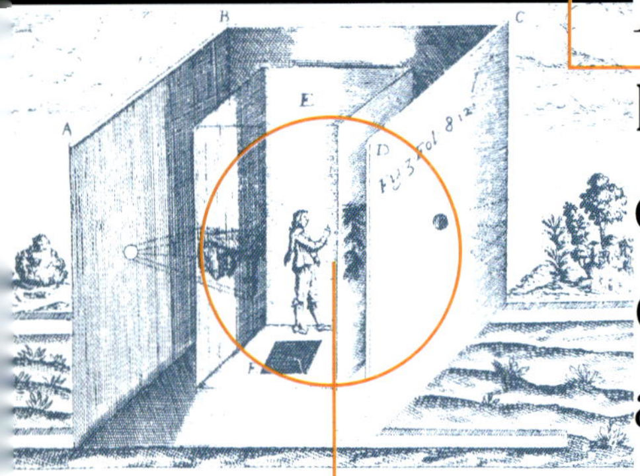

From the introduction of the *camera obscura* as a tool for observation and drawing to the growth of human sciences during the seventeenth and eighteenth centuries, a mosaic of ideas, discoveries and devices came together to change the way we view ourselves and the world. Photography was not discovered suddenly but rather emerged as a result of several centuries of scientific and artistic explorations into light, optics and perception. By the nineteenth century, photography's primary role was to record and support many existing ideas and scientific theories of the day.

In Latin, *camera* means *room* or *chamber* and *obscura* means *dark*. It was discovered that an image could be seen projected through a small opening onto an opposite wall in a dark room or tent. By the 1500s, there were working models of the *camera obscura*, which more than two centuries later would enable the invention of photography.

The Murex bandaris snail taught the ancient Greeks and Romans about the light-sensitivity of certain materials. The purpura snail was used to dye fabric because its secretions turned a rich purple when exposed to sunlight.

First invented in China, spectacles did not appear in the West until the middle of the thirteenth century.

Opticks

Best known for his concept of gravity, Isaac Newton also invented calculus and formulated the basic laws of motion and optics.

While staying at his mother's estate to avoid the Great Plague sweeping through England, Newton formed his theories and produced the first scientific work about light based on experimentation. He turned one room of the house into a *camera obscura,* focusing sunlight through two prisms to **prove** that white light contained all the colors of the spectrum.

Newton was 23 when he began to develop his theories of light, though it would be more than thirty years before his pioneering book, *Opticks*, was published in 1704.

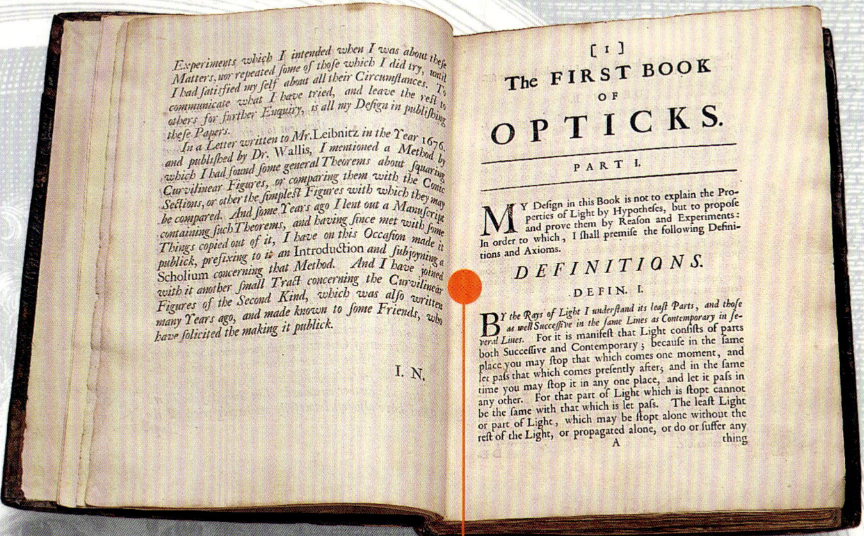

Experiments which I intended when I was about these Matters, nor repeated some of those which I did try, until I had satisfied my self about all their Circumstances. To communicate what I have tried, and leave the rest to others for further Enquiry, is all my Design in publishing these Papers.

In a Letter written to Mr. Leibnitz *in the Year 1676. and published by Dr.* Wallis, *I mentioned a Method by which I had found some general Theorems about squaring Curvilinear Figures, or comparing them with the Conic Sections, or other the simplest Figures with which they may be compared. And some Years ago I lent out a Manuscript containing such Theorems, and having since met with some Things copied out of it, I have on this Occasion made it publick, prefixing to it an* Introduction *and subjoyning a* Scholium *concerning that Method. And I have joined with it another small Tract concerning the Curvilinear Figures of the Second Kind, which was also written many Years ago, and made known to some Friends, who have solicited the making it publick.*

I. N.

[1]

The FIRST BOOK OF OPTICKS.

PART I.

My Design in this Book is not to explain the Properties of Light by Hypotheses, but to propose and prove them by Reason and Experiments: In order to which, I shall premise the following Definitions and Axioms.

DEFINITIONS.

DEFIN. I.

B*y the Rays of Light I understand its least Parts, and those as well Successive in the same Lines as Contemporary in several Lines.* For it is manifest that Light consists of parts both Successive and Contemporary; because in the same place you may stop that which comes one moment, and let pass that which comes presently after; and in the same time you may stop it in any one place, and let it pass in any other. For that part of Light which is stopt cannot be the same with that which is let pass. The least Light or part of Light, which may be stopt alone without the rest of the Light, or propagated alone, or do or suffer any

A thing

In 1642, Galileo died and Isaac Newton was born.

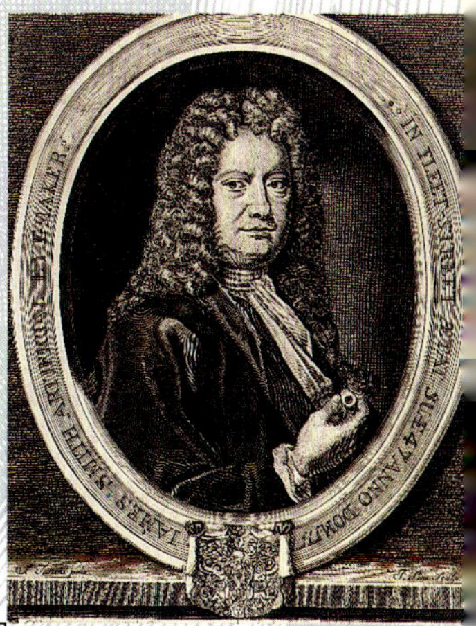

Toward the invention of photography

As the Scientific Revolution dawned in the 1700s, ancient methods and theories were replaced with a new approach to science based on **observation** and **experimentation**. Newton's study of optics led to the improvement of devices such as telescopes and microscopes and greatly expanded people's understanding of otherwise invisible worlds. Newton's innovative model of exploration set the standard for all the sciences.

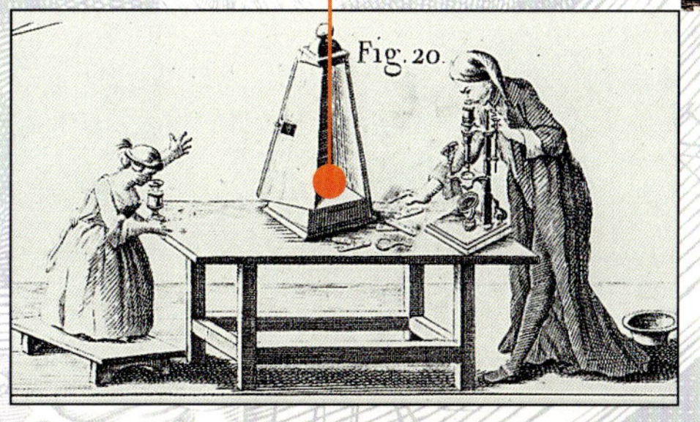

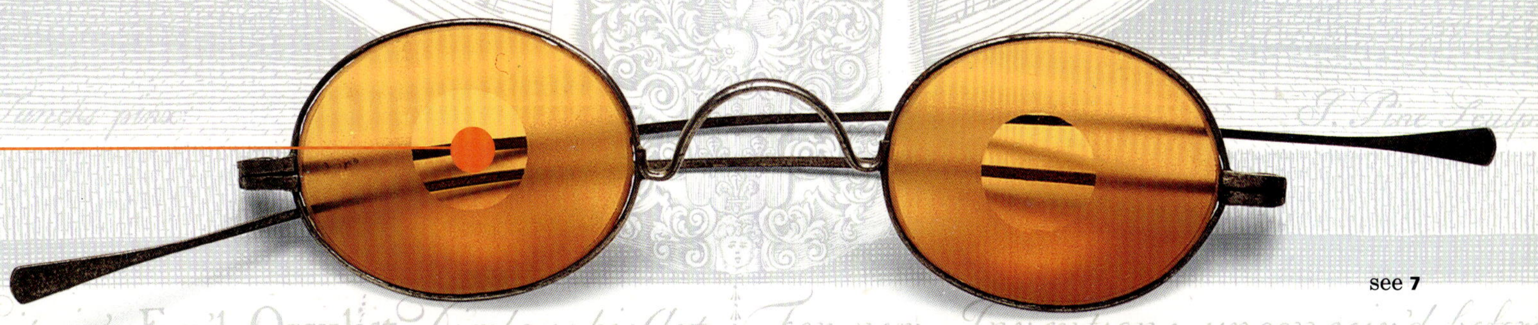

see 7

Britain's Fam'd Occulist Displays his Art For new Inventions, unconceiv'd before

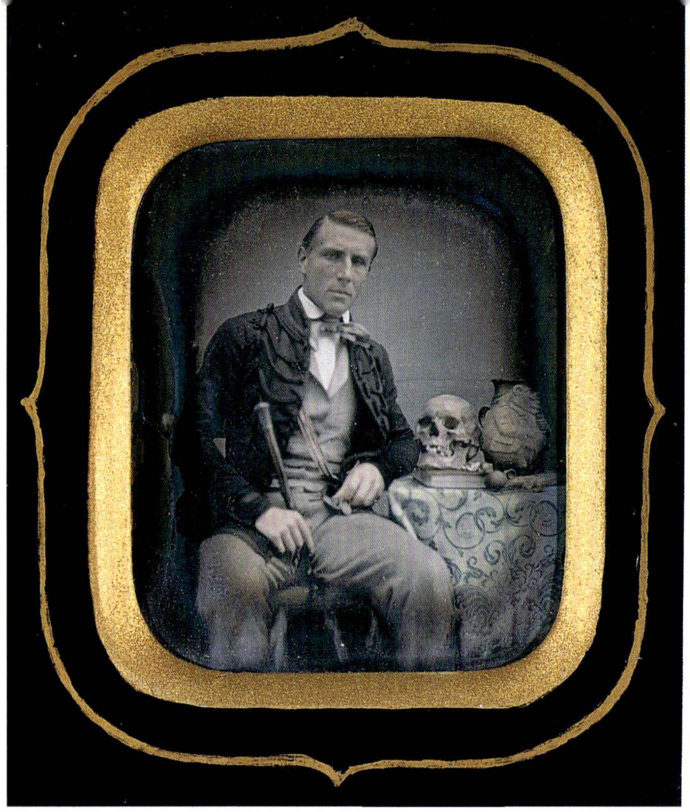

Art and science worked together

in developing tools of observation, allowing artists to depict nature in a realistic way that was not previously possible.

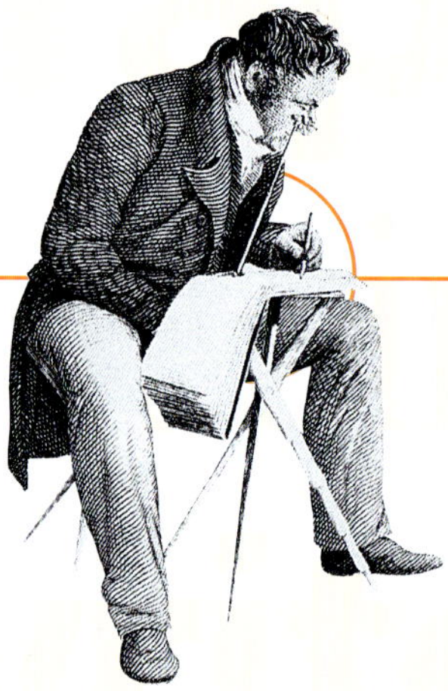

Sir John Herschel, an important contributor to the early development of photography, was an astronomer, physicist and chemist. Throughout his life he utilized the *camera lucida* as a drawing tool to make both art and observations. Herschel invented the cyanotype process, discovered the use of hyposulfites (hypo) for stabilizing sensitized paper, introduced the terms *negative* and *positive* and was one of the first to use the word *photography*.

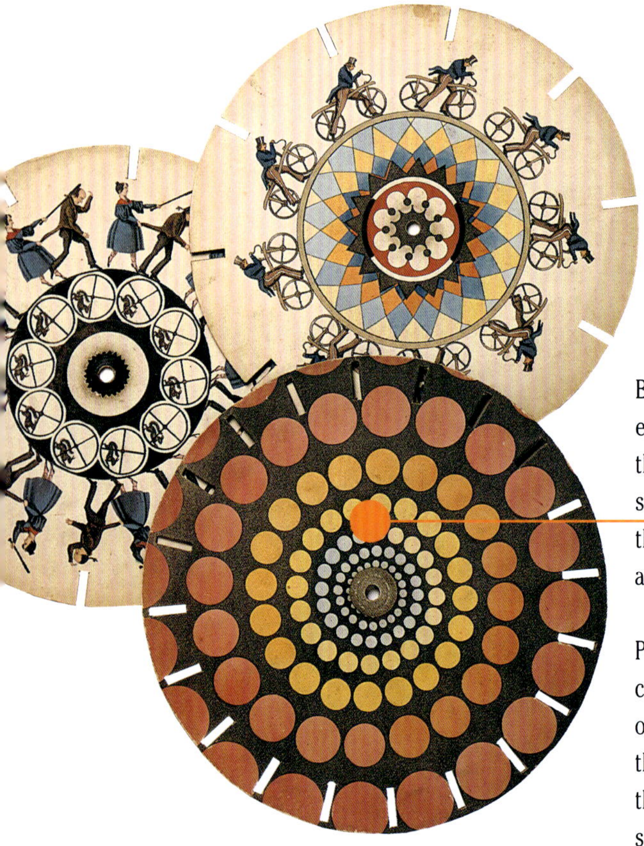

By the late-1700s, tracing devices such as the *camera obscura* and *camera lucida* were in everyday use. Studies of the eye led to an understanding of **persistence of vision**, the eye's ability to perceive a series of still images as continuous motion. Optical devices such as the phenakistascope (the Greek *phenaz* means *deceiver,* and *scopein* means *to see*), the *thaumatrope* (Greek for "*turning wonder*"), and the *zoetrope* (*zoa* means *living things* and *trope* means *turning*) became popular forms of entertainment.

Photography was invented out of this climate of investigation and exploration. It was not coincidence that brought several people independently to the brink of discovering a method of making an image by sunlight. All of the pieces of the photographic puzzle were in place: the light sensitivity of certain substances, the camera already in use as a drawing tool, and the *desire* to make a permanent fixed image by light. With several centuries of art and science in place, photography was invented and embraced by both the scientific and artistic world. Two ancient Greek words were combined to create a word for the new invention, **photos** meaning **light** and **graphein** meaning **to write**.

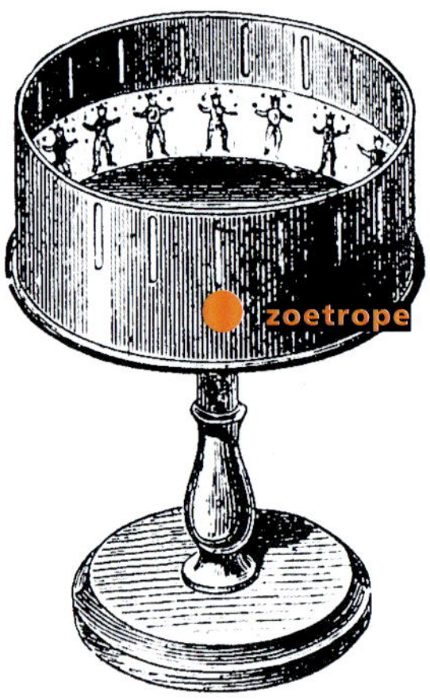

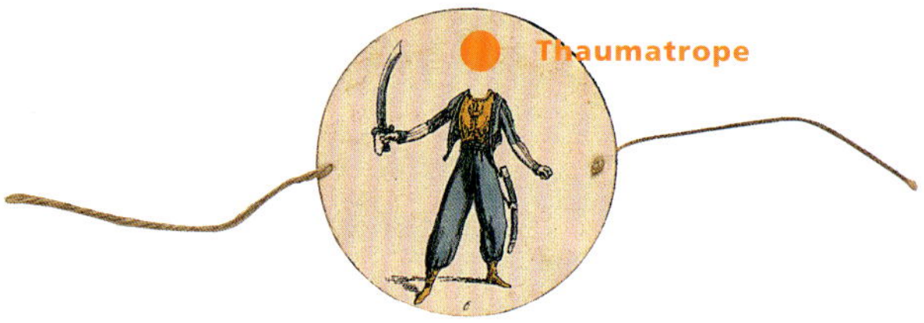

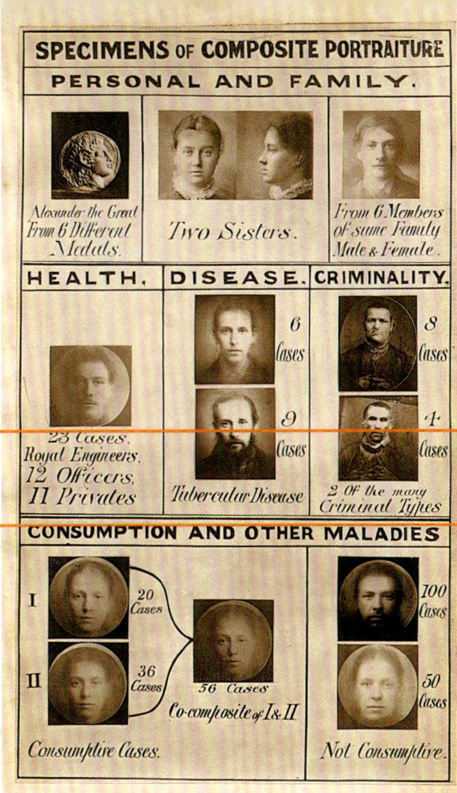

The Archive

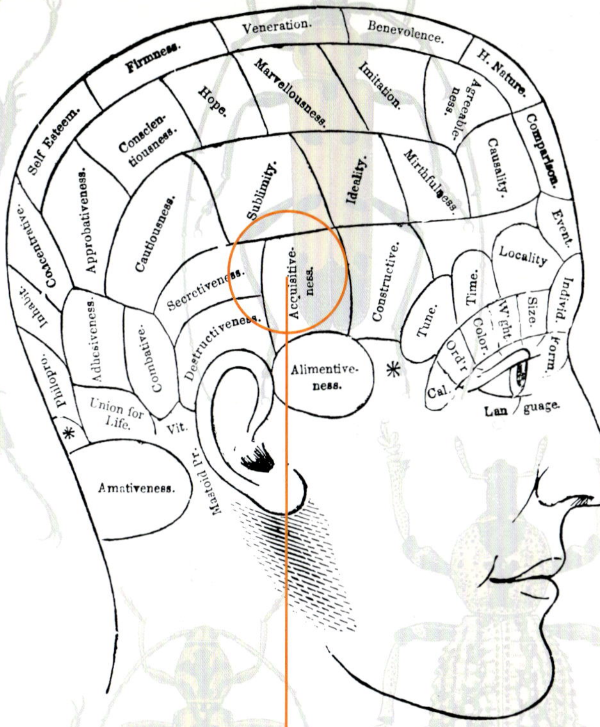

The desire to classify and provide taxonomic order to the world—whether it was fossils, plants, insects or the human animal—had become a primary function of the sciences in the nineteenth century. From the study of human emotions to the classification of emotional types, photography quickly became a valuable tool in the "scientific" support of these new ideas and theories.

In the pursuit of human sciences, the brain provided the largest unknown territory to decipher. Phrenology—the reading of the bumps on the head and the shape of the skull to determine the character, intelligence and race of an individual—was one aspect in this classification of the Nature of Man.

Photography also played an important role in the cataloging of criminals as police work became more of a science. It was hoped that the photographic archiving of criminals could be used not only for identification but also as a means of determining a criminal type based on physical features such as the size and shape of the ears and the shape of a person's forehead.

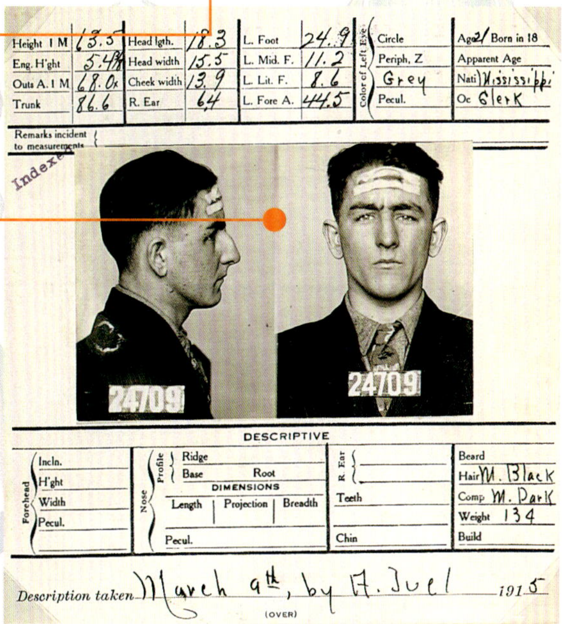

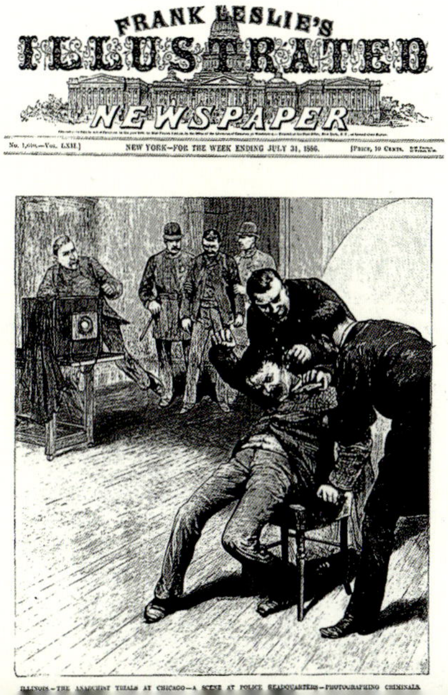

Invented during a time of discovery and advancement in optics, light and technology, photography quickly became a primary tool for both scientists and artists as they explored new ways to relate to the world. Today, as we continue to discover new technologies and new insights into previously invisible worlds, photography still plays a key role in our awareness and understanding of visual culture.

Special thanks to Robert Shimshak and Mike and Patty Kramer for opening their collections to the editors.

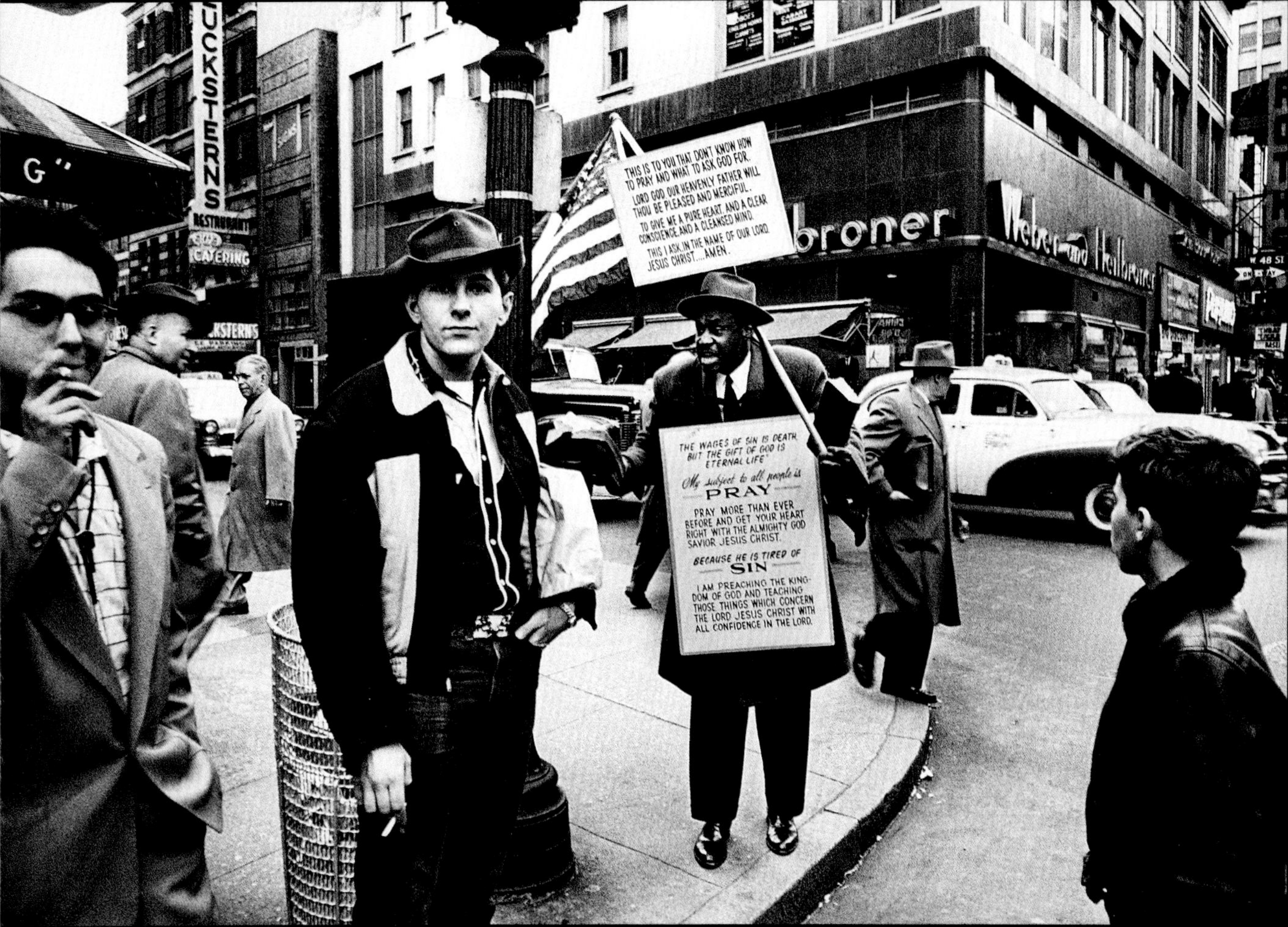

William Klein, "Pray & Sin," 1955, silver print 20" X 24"

Available work by: **Jeanne Dunning**
Doug Hall
Biff Henrich
William Klein
Wright Morris
Margaret Moulton
Thomas Sicurella

FAZAL SHEIKH

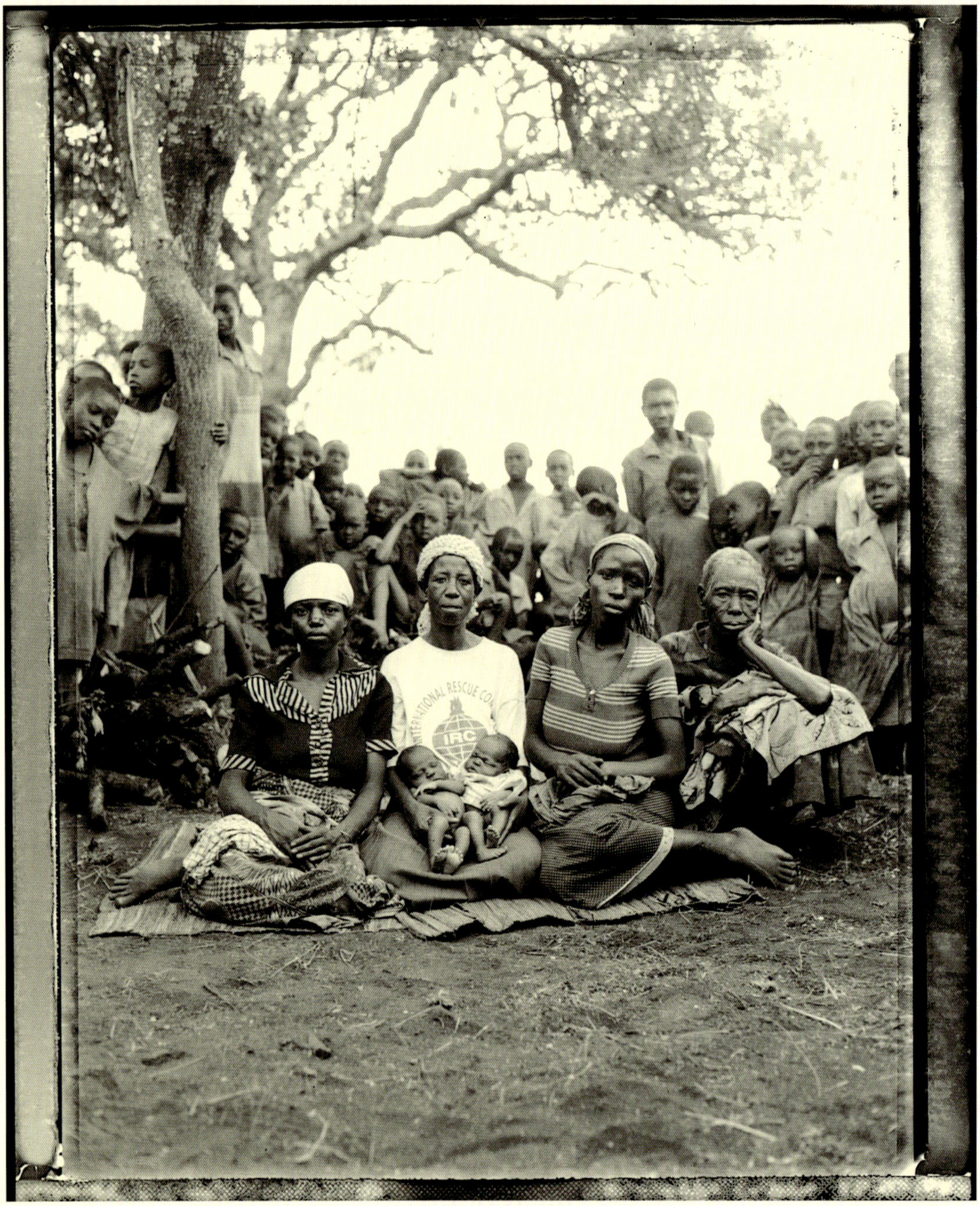

Traditional Birthing Attendant, Nyabahire Esteri holding newborns Nsabimana ("I beg something from God") and Mukanzabonimpa ("God will give me, but I don't know when") with their mothers Kanyange, Mukabatazi and Mukabatazi's mother, Rwandan refugee camp, Lumasi, Tanzania, 1994.

I WORK TO OFFSET OR PROVIDE A BALANCE to the imagery that foregrounds visions of Africa as a mythic Dark Continent. I choose to make direct, unmanipulated renderings of the people and their home. It is my sense that by expanding our visual representations of Africa we can arrive at a level of understanding, empathy and commonality that will bring about changes in stereotypical perceptions. Then, when we see and hear the five-line blip of news on the television, we are more aware that this only scratches at the surface of a situation that has many more layers. —Fazal Sheikh

Facing page: ***Mama Nyiramugna, Rwandan refugee camp, Lumasi, Tanzania, 1994.***

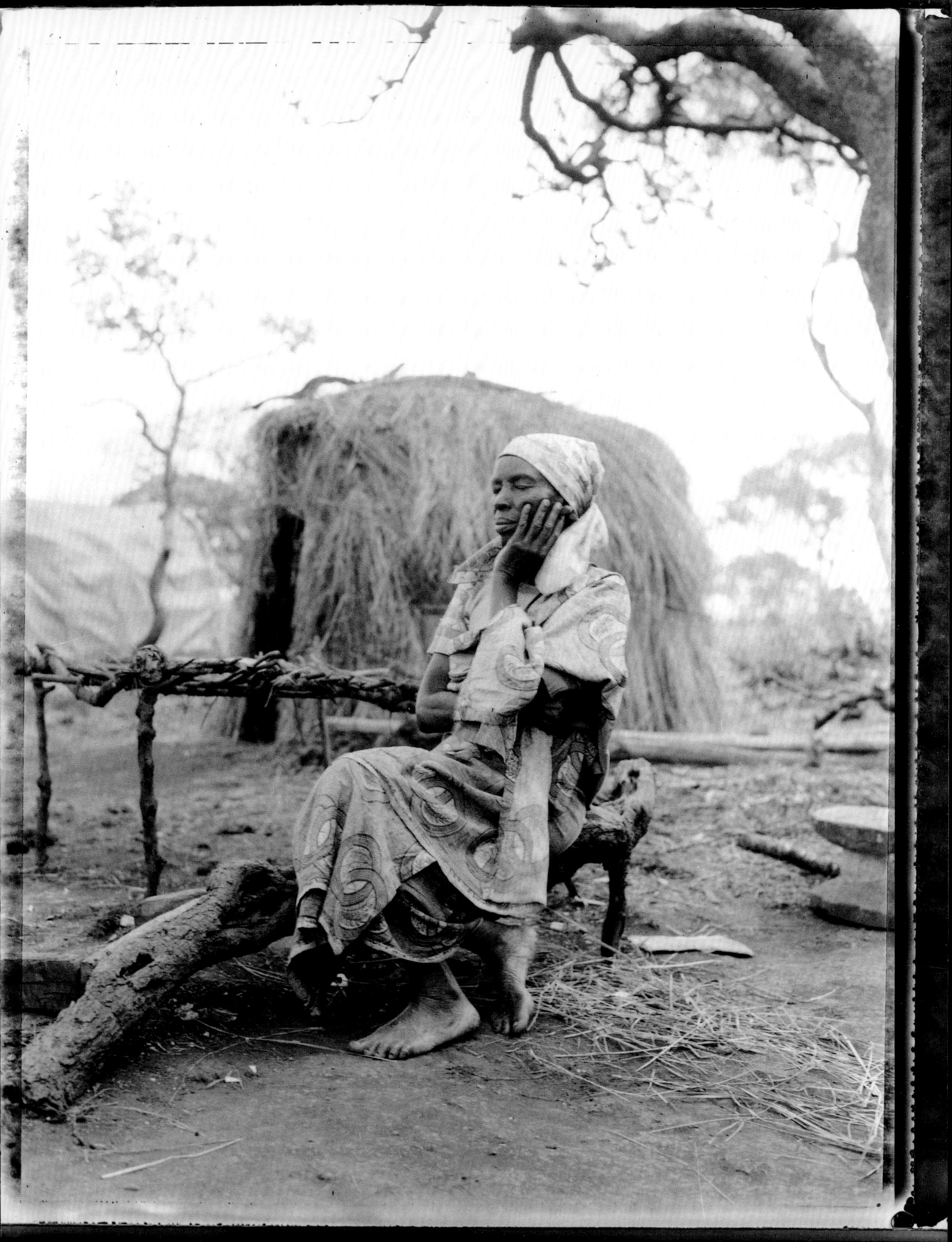

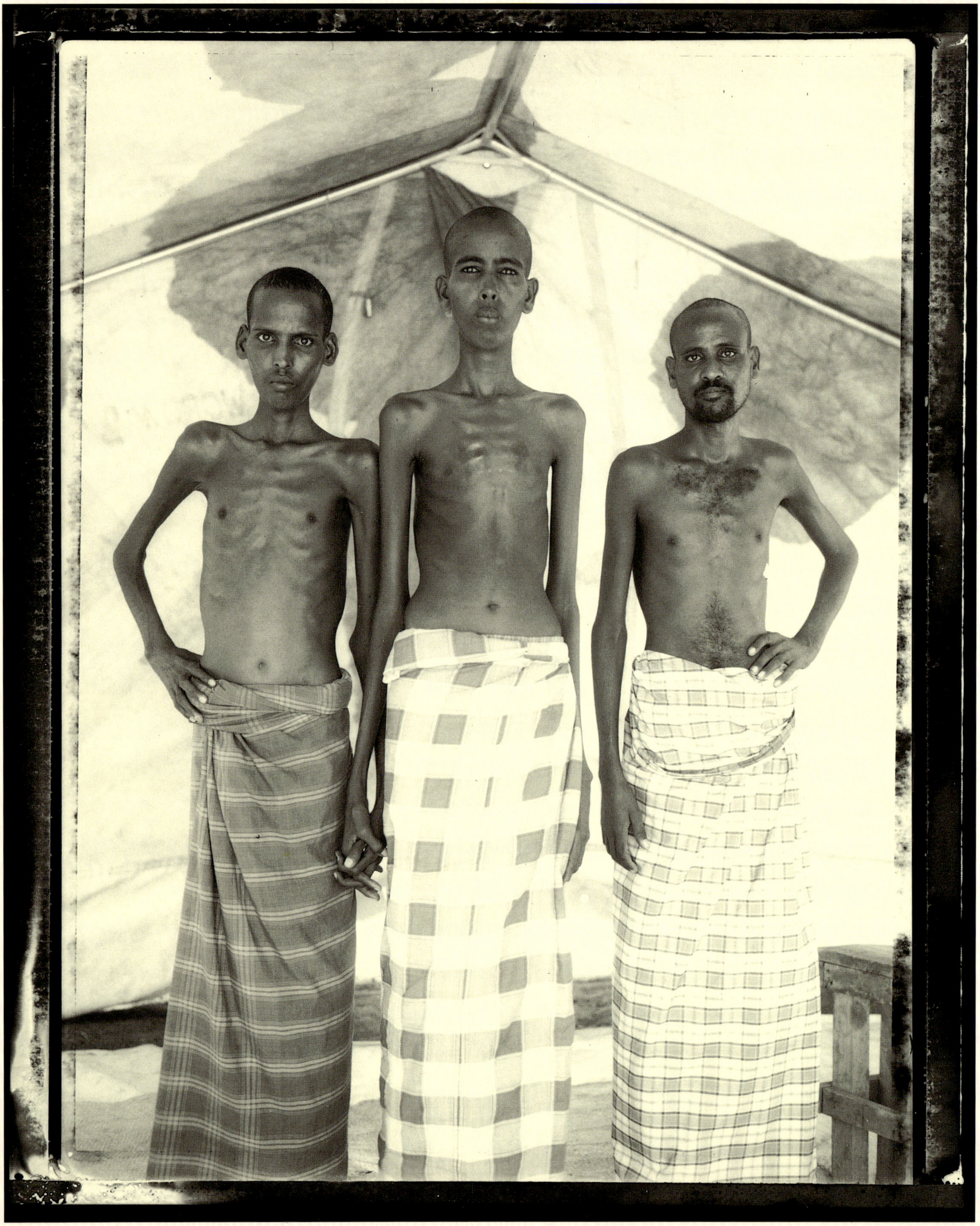

Tuberculosis Ward, Somali refugee camp, Mandera, Kenya, 1993.

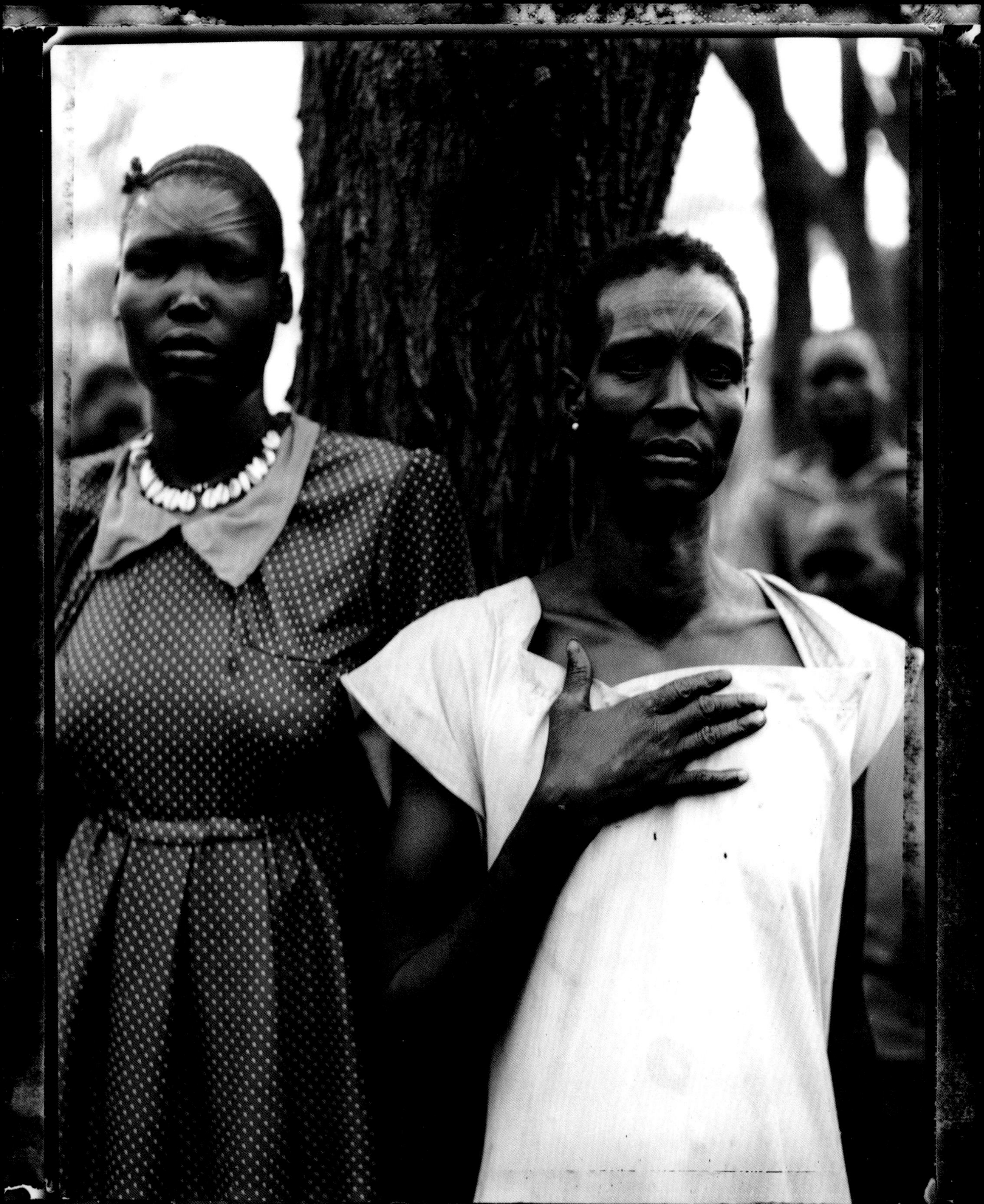

Ajoh Achot and Achol Manyen, family section, Sudanese refugee camp, Lokichoggio, Kenya, 1992–93.

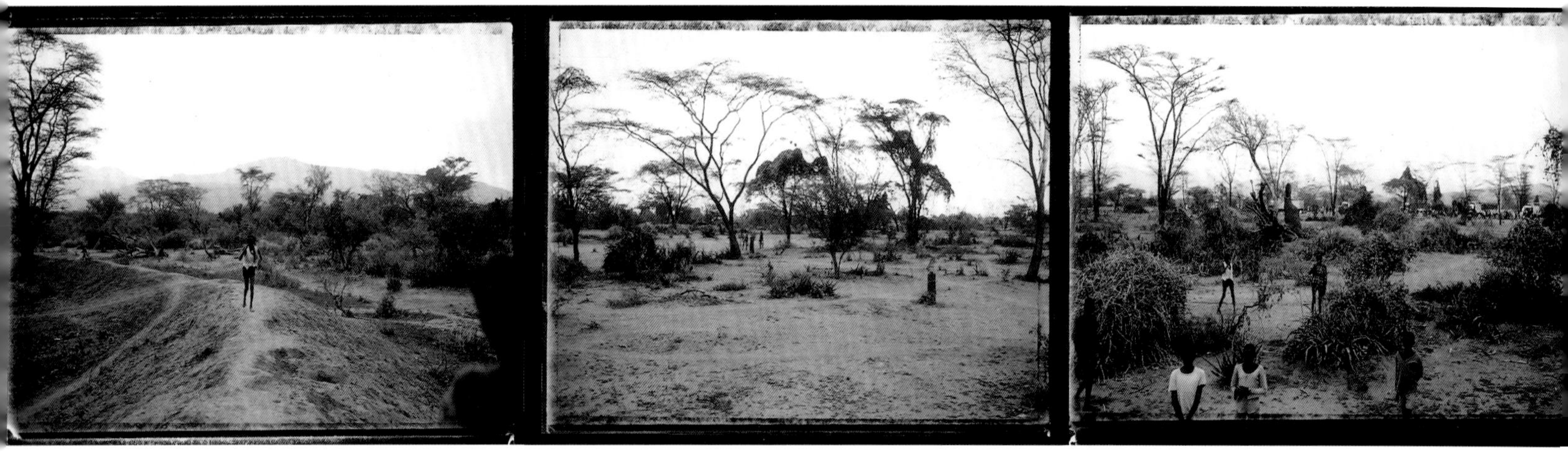

Sudanese Refugee Camp, Lokichoggio, Kenya, Sudanese hills to the left. Truck loading at dawn for transport of Sudanese Minors to more permanent settlement at Kakuma, Kenya, **1992.**

Below: ***Sudanese Refugee Camp, Lokichoggio, Kenya, "Unaccompanied Minors" morning of departure to new refugee camp further south within the Kenyan borders,*** **1992.**

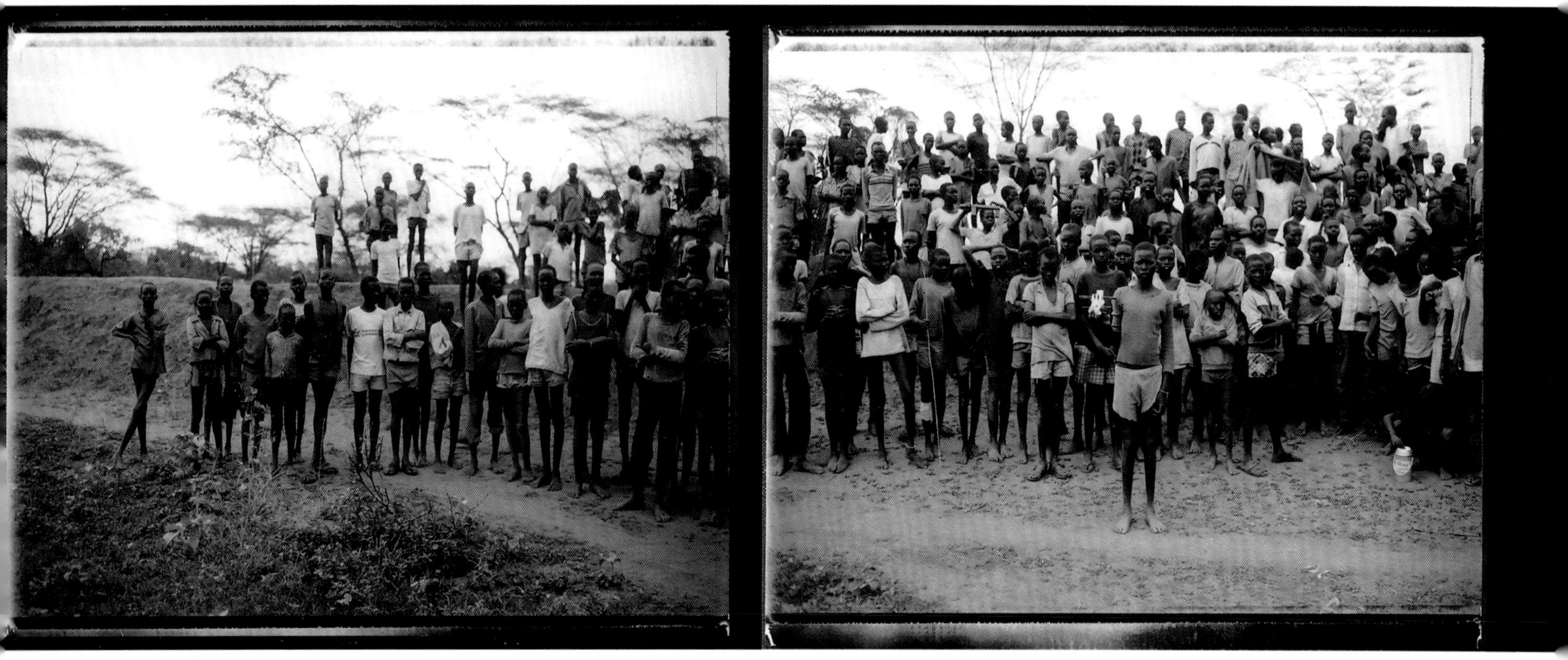

A PRAYER FOR THE LIVING

BY CARLA WILLIAMS

Outsider, insider—does it matter who makes the image? It matters what the motives are.

In Fazal Sheikh's photographs of Sudanese, Ethiopian, Somali, Mozambican and Rwandan people living in refugee camps in eastern Africa, the motive is to dispense information in a fair light, to offer an alternative to the invasive and sensationalistic depictions that Western journalists routinely offer us of such situations. While first-person anecdotes enliven and flesh out, and statistics sober and inform, neither provides complete representation. Two things are apparent when I look at these photographs and think of the places from which they come: there is more living going on here than we think, and every one of the images is its own rich, multifarious narrative.

300,000; 500,000; two million; ten million—I cannot conceive of these numbers in any real terms that apply to me. All I know is that whatever they represent in human terms, it is gravely serious. What does it mean for a country when one-third of the population either is killed or literally gets up and walks out? What does it mean for the people in the place they must adopt as their new home? And who is facilitating in all of this?

By definition, these refugee camps are not the end of the journey but rather the entrenchment between battles—the deep, drawn breath before exhalation. This life is war—as epic, destructive and apocalyptic as any that has been, fought hand-to-hand against one's neighbor, his blood draining off into the dirt at your feet.

Sheikh's photographs possess a patina and formality generally associated with a nineteenth-century tradition of portraiture, demanding the utmost care in the rendering of the subject and relying upon his or her complicity in making it successful. Sheikh never poses his subjects, nor does he assume that a document cannot first be a portrait, richly rendered to heighten its authority and command a presence in the world. The tonality of the prints—sometimes muted, sometimes graphic—recalls the very color of the earth and the light of the place. Yet these people exist right here, right now, separated not temporally but by distance, geography. There can be nothing nostalgic about the never-before-seen, about subjects as they present themselves, often for the first time, to the camera: conscious but not self-conscious, fully possessed of the solemnity of the record-making event. You do not have to be photographed every day—or ever, for that matter—to understand your physical being and its presence, to comport yourself accordingly. Like the disenfranchised in Walker Evans' or Doris Ullman's work, no one here seems to smile, and the viewer is disarmed. For it is a smile that we crave, a hint, an ever-so-slightly turned up corner of a lip that in our minds reassures us that it isn't so bad, that *everything's going to be okay,* that they really are like us.

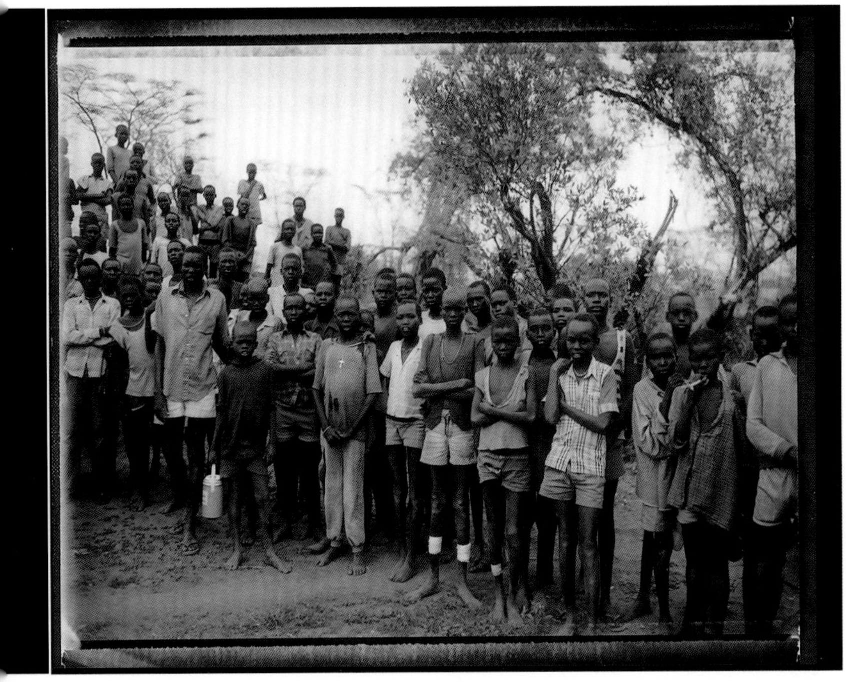

12,000 boys, now assembled, now scattered, like 8- to 18-year-olds often are. They are believed to be faceless, like all homeless persons—as if stability and rootedness are required to make you visible, viable. And yet they are here and standing to be recorded just as plainly as anyone. The format of the panoramic triptych mimics the reality of the so-called "unaccompanied minors" perpetually moving across the continent. Their continual journey through the land, and their existence on it and in it, transforms them into whichever place currently claims them. They are displaced from their homeland, many perhaps believing that it *will* all be over one day, and they will be moving on, going home, getting well.

These photographs encompass, in the mutual reverence and honesty between subject and photographer, the truths about the place, the experience of making the pictures, and the individual identities of the subjects. They allow individuals whose lives and stories are represented to declare their very existence and demand their recognition. Can we come away knowing these people, because we have stared at them and learned their names? Of course not. We come away knowing *of* them, what they have presented of themselves to the photographer and, by extension, to us.

Framing Politics

THE IMAGE-CONSCIOUS TURN IN PHOTOJOURNALISM

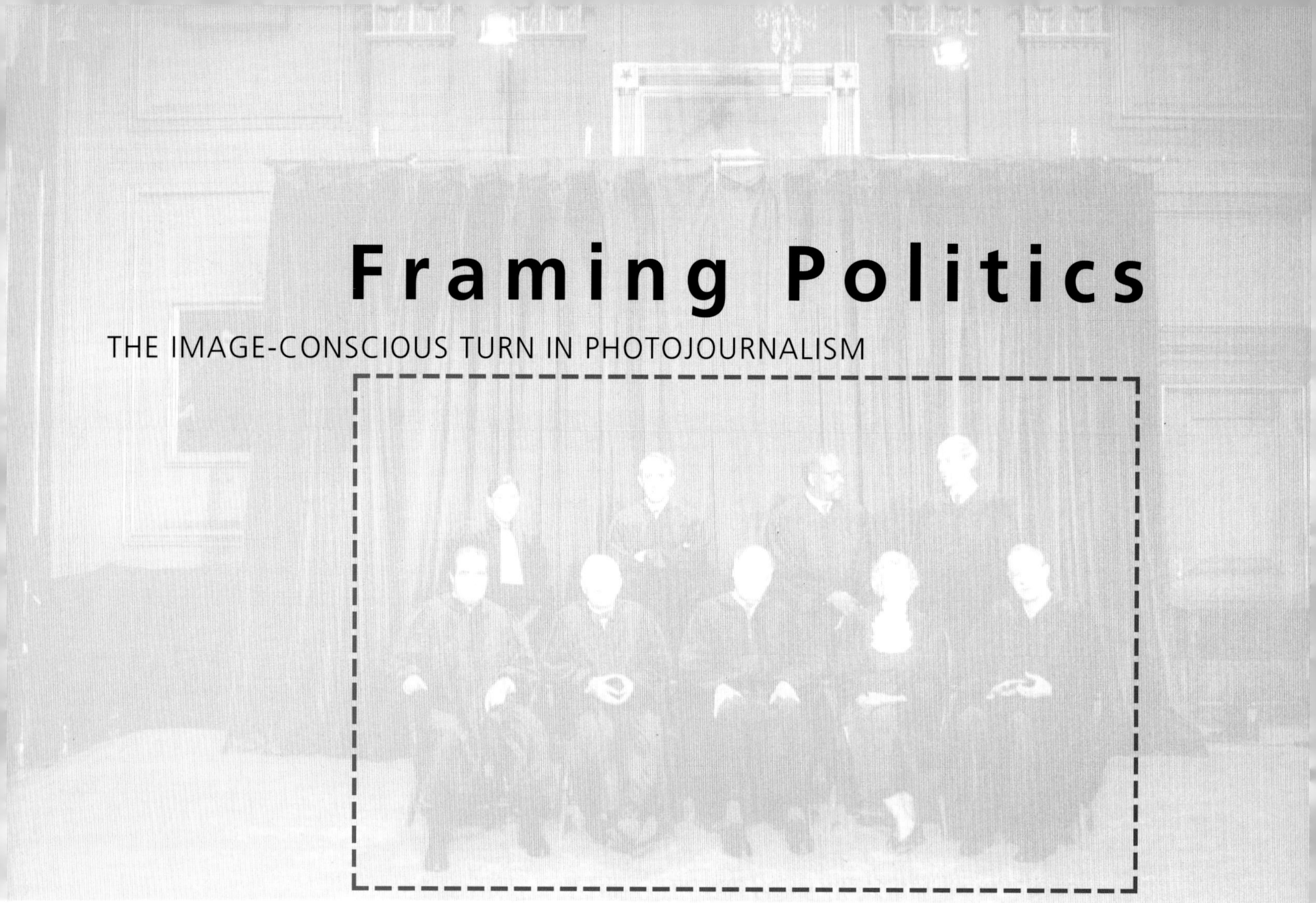

Straight from the wire. Stephen Crowley/NYT Pictures.

BY KIKU ADATTO

PUBLIC
IMAGES

The annual portrait of the justices of the Supreme Court is not usually worthy of note, but last November's photograph in the *New York Times* is no ordinary picture. Instead of the traditional dignified pose, we see the trappings of a photo session laid bare: the justices are viewed from a distance, framed by a large curtained backdrop in a room that has been rearranged and lit for the camera. They are caught unaware in the act of posing.

Why was this picture in the paper? And why have similar photos begun to appear in the *Times* and other newspapers? The answer has less to do with any policy or explicit decision by photographers and editors than with a larger story about the rise of a new image consciousness in American life. The image-conscious sensibility that is shaping photojournalism today has its origins in the world of art photography some three or four decades ago.

PICTURES ABOUT PICTURES

CONSIDER GARRY WINOGRAND'S 1960 photograph of John Kennedy addressing the Democratic National Convention. The picture is composed of three elements. In the foreground is a small portable television framing Kennedy's head as he delivers his speech. In the middle ground stands the gesticulating candidate, his back to the camera. In the background, out of focus, is a bank of television cameras. With this equation, Winogrand directs our attention from politics to the pose, from the political event to the irony of political form. He was not interested in the meaning of the event as it is experienced by the participants, but in the meaning of the scene as a picture about pictures.

Winogrand's approach signaled a departure from the traditional ambitions both of documentary and art photography. Typically, documentary photography aimed to reveal and record reality, while art photography interpreted it. By the late-1950s, however, art photographers began to direct the viewer's attention to a reality beyond the subject of the photograph. They focused on the image as an image, as artifice, as an act of fabrication. They also self-consciously explored their own role in the image-making process, as did Lee Friedlander in *Self Portrait,* a book of urban scenes in which the photographer's shadow or reflection appear in every frame.

Perhaps the most famous example of this new image-consciousness is the pop art of Andy Warhol. With mind-numbing repetition, Warhol reproduced the most potent news images—race riots, a mourning Jacqueline Kennedy, car crashes—as if calling attention to the effects of the television instant replay. Moreover, his multiple images of Campbell's soup cans, Brillo pads, Marilyn Monroe and other icons of popular culture direct our attention away from the subject matter towards the instruments of image-making: the frame, the packaging, the pose.

IMAGE-CONSCIOUS NEWS

TELEVISION NEWS in the 1960s was immune to these developments in the art world. Television reporters, led by Walter Cronkite and Huntley and Brinkley, still had more in common with Edward Murrow than MoMA. Steeped in the tradition of print journalism, television reporters concentrated on what public figures said and did, not on how their images were crafted for the media. It wasn't until 1988, in the wake of the Reagan presidency, that image-consciousness finally invaded television news. As political campaigns mastered the art of television image-making, reporters shifted from recording the words of the candidates to exposing their images and revealing their contrivances. The news began to read like Andy Warhol's pop art, repeatedly displaying the candidates' ads, media events and media gurus.

With the 1992 presidential campaign, the networks made an effort to stem the tide of image-conscious reporting. Inspired by the "ad watches" developed by print journalists and local television stations, the nightly news focused more attention on political issues and examined the veracity of candidates' ads instead of running them uncritically. Yet, even as television news struggled to overcome its preoccupation with image-making, the image-conscious sensibility found a new home in the very place that had long eschewed it: the pages of the *New York Times.* During the '90s, the *Times* has devoted many news reports to the way politicians craft images for television, and its news photographs increasingly resemble the image-conscious style of art photographers.

Photojournalists of the '90s are not consciously imitating art photographers any more than television reporters did during the '80s; photographers and their editors merely are looking for interesting pictures. Today, the image-conscious sensibility has seeped so deeply into our popular and political culture that showing "pictures of pictures" has become a familiar aesthetic.

Decades earlier, it was a startling idea.

The news began to read like Andy Warhol's pop art, repeatedly displaying the candidates' ads, media events and media gurus.

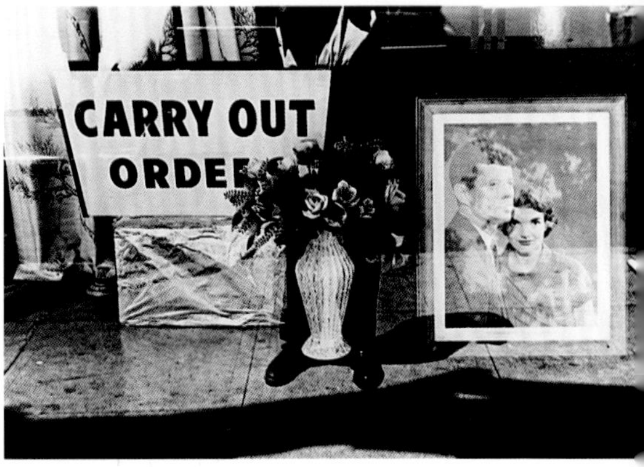

Lee Friedlander, *Washington, D.C.,* 1962. Courtesy Fraenkel Gallery, San Francisco.

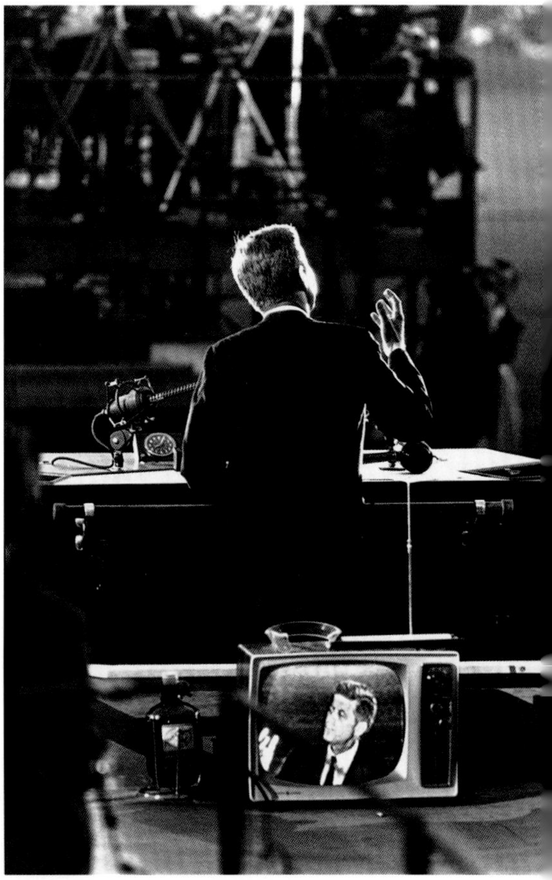

Garry Winogrand, *Democratic National Convention,* 1960. Courtesy Fraenkel Gallery, San Francisco. © Estate of Garry Winogrand.

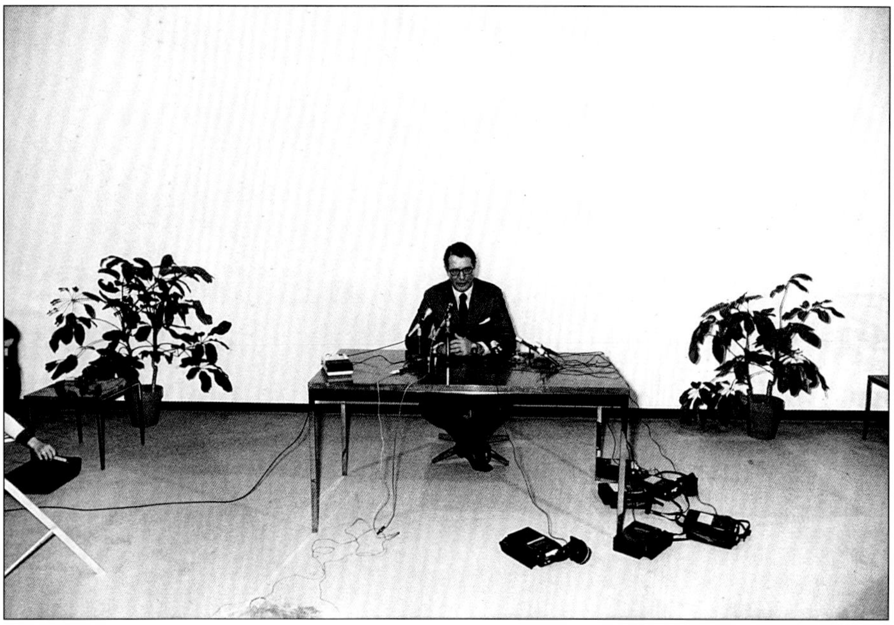

Garry Winogrand, *Elliot Richardson Press Conference, Austin*, 1973. Courtesy Fraenkel Gallery, San Francisco. © Estate of Garry Winogrand.

REPORTERS AND PHOTOGRAPHERS AS PERFORMERS IN THE FRAME

IN 1977, WINOGRAND PUBLISHED a series of photographs of media events titled *Public Relations.* The book's cover features a picture of Elliot Richardson, who, impeccably dressed, would look the picture of poise in a standard news photograph. Winogrand's wide-angle shot, however, makes him look oddly isolated in the stage-like room. A white wall looms behind Richardson, and two incongruous house plants flank his makeshift conference desk. The symmetry of the odd scene is upset only by a reporter poking her head into the side of the frame to adjust her tape recorder. In *Public Relations,* Winogrand is not content merely to undermine the poses of politicians; he also implicates photographers and reporters in the artifice of the events they record. Far from being out of the frame, they are framed themselves—sometimes sedately poised in the foreground of the photograph, other times jostling for position in a chaos of pointing microphones and cameras.

Today, we are aware as never before of the artifice that constitutes the pose. We are as fascinated by how images are made as we are by what they mean.

Similarly, a photograph of Robert Dole that appeared last November in the *Times* exposes the self-conscious choreography of press and politicians. Like Elliot Richardson, Robert Dole has constructed a pose for the cameras. With hands purposefully clasped, he leans attentively towards a photographer crouched on the floor. Despite Dole's attempt to control his image, the *Times* photograph makes his office look like a set, framed by a photographer's curtain. Dole's constructed pose is deconstructed, as is the "pose" of the "official" photographer absorbed in his craft.

FAILED IMAGES: FRAMING THE FLAW

TO CALL ATTENTION to the picture as a picture is a way of puncturing its intended meaning. Since the '50s, art photographers increasingly used what would be considered mistakes in conventional photography—the misplacement of the central figure, people caught in odd poses or out-of-focus, heads jutting into the frame—to subvert the conventional picture.

In his influential 1958 book, *The Americans,* Robert Frank used this technique to reveal truths that the idealized images of post-war America attempted to conceal. Watching a parade in Hoboken, New Jersey, Frank turned his camera away from the flags and festivities to photograph the onlookers. One of Frank's images depicts two women watching a parade from their perch in a dingy building. Rather than glorify the American flag that dominates the photograph, Frank shows it as a misshapen and mournful emblem that blocks the women's view of the parade and our view of them.

Similarly, a photographic mistake—the blurred figure of a woman in the foreground of the shot, surrounded by an attentive group of spectators—is used in a 1993 *Times* photograph to reframe the event and subvert its conventional meaning. Without reading the caption, it is impossible to tell what this photograph is about. Who is the woman in the foreground of the picture, her head cut off by the photographer's frame? The caption does not identify her. She serves as a foil for the photographer, a means of disrupting the political event and distracting our attention from the politicians featured in the story: Senator Harris Wofford and Representative Christopher Shays. As in the popular children's book *Where's Waldo?,* you have to search for the main character in the confusing scenery.

THE SELF DEFORMED

THE EYE FOR THE FLAW that deconstructs the pose is also the eye that deforms the self. Diane Arbus used deformity—both real and imposed by the camera—as a metaphor, a means of subverting normalcy. "You see someone on the street and essentially what you notice is the flaw," observed Arbus. "If you scrutinize reality closely enough, if in some way you really, really get to it, it becomes fantastic."

Arbus used her camera to transform her subjects into strange caricatures of themselves. In a photograph titled "Boy with a straw hat waiting to march in a pro-war parade, N.Y.C., 1967," a young man stares primly at the camera. In Arbus' hands, his pose is made to mock his ideals. She used flash not to document but to cast an air of unreality on the scene, making symbols like the American flag and patriotic buttons look like props.

For her photograph "A Jewish giant with his parents in the Bronx, New York, 1970," Arbus took shot after shot before she achieved the absurd juxtaposition she sought. The labelling of the photograph underscores the depersonalization of her subjects, her insistence on directing our attention to the odd violations of social categories and expectations.

An eye for the absurd, for creating deformity to undermine convention, also characterizes a photograph of President Clinton that appeared in the *Times* in July 1993. The photograph's caption exposes the President's intent to use "the White House stage to promote the earned-income credit." Shot from an extreme low angle with a wide-angle lens, Clinton looms, like Diane Arbus' giant, over the families seated on stage. The accompanying news report reiterates the photograph's message: "The flowers were fake, the books borrowed and the stiff poses could have been borrowed from *Family Feud.* But the faux-homey set on a White House stage had a real political purpose." This "purpose," however, is not the point of the photograph. The picture instead is a pun on the artifice of the media event.

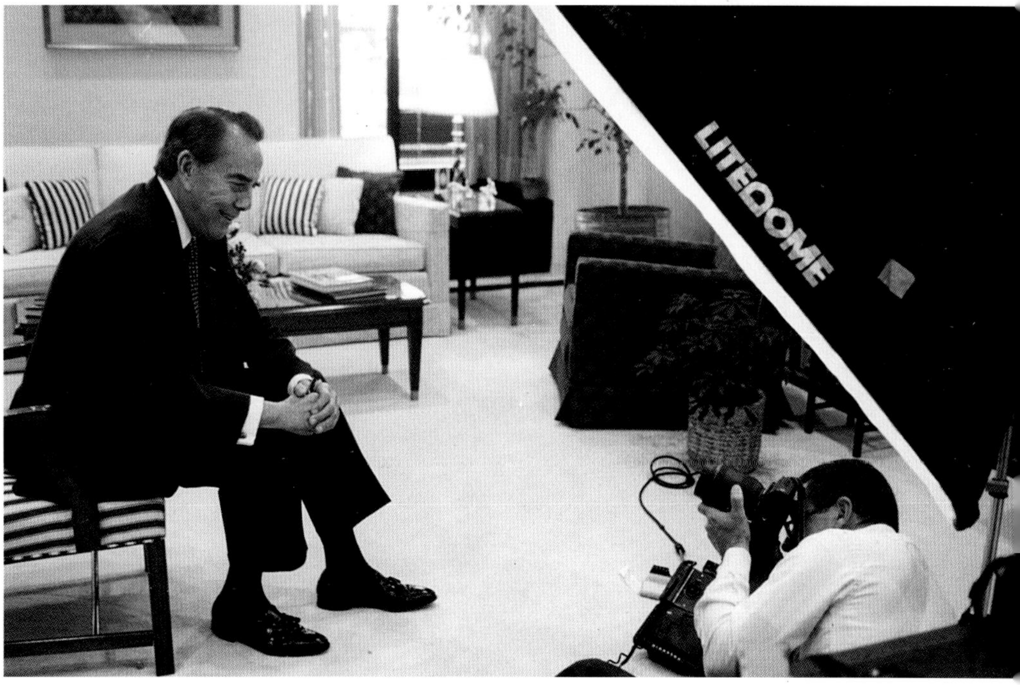

AP/Wide World Photos.

THE UNRAVELING OF RITUAL

TODAY, WE ARE AWARE as never before of the artifice that constitutes the pose. We are as fascinated by how images are made as we are by what they mean. This is evident not only in art photography, television news and photojournalism but also in the image-conscious sensibility that pervades advertising, MTV and the hip self-consciousness of *Seinfeld,* David Letterman's *The Late Show* and even best-selling children's books, which now call attention to the conventions of storytelling.

What should we make of this turn in our culture? The skepticism that underlies image consciousness is an important corrective to cant and puffery, and to myths that exempt established conventions from critical examination. But there also are limits to this form of critique, which are particularly relevant to news reporting and photojournalism. Does image-conscious journalism break through illusions and extricate the public from the manipulation of the media? Or is it merely a sophisticated trap, a hall of mirrors, in which photographers and reporters remain entangled in the artifice they mean to expose?

For all its virtues as a form of critique, the image-conscious perspective is limited in important ways. It distracts us from paying attention to the content of the primary event and to the meanings it conveys. Also, the technique often settles simply to expose the artifice in image-making. Still, the fact that an image is contrived for the cameras does not make it false. The distinction between real and pseudo-events must be judged not on the method of presentation, but on the content of the event itself. The pose is only part of the story. For reporters and photojournalists to fixate on the pose is to rest with revealing artifice instead of moving to the truth that lies beyond.

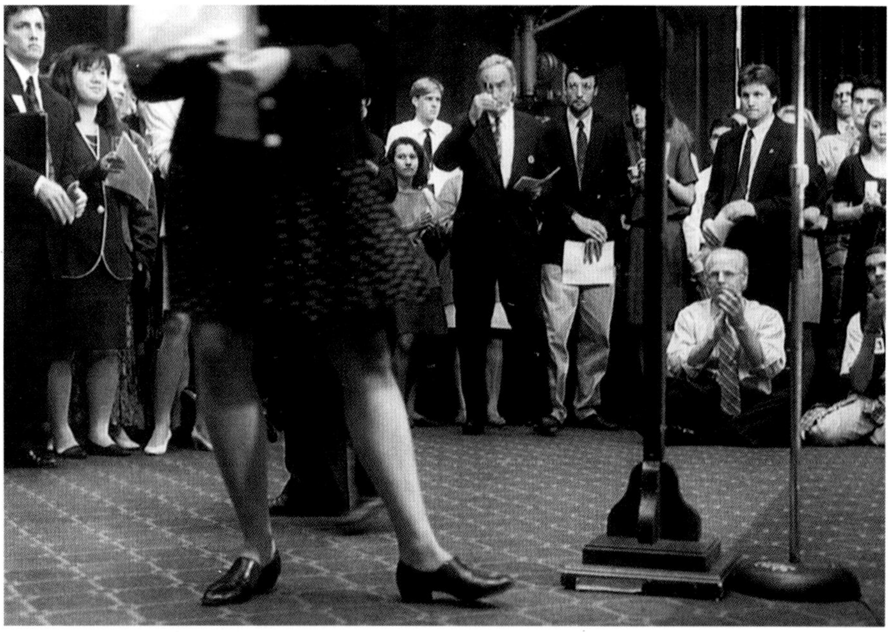

Stephen Crowley/NYT Pictures.

Rise and Fall of the New West

BY C.P. ROSENTHAL

"Paul de Man is dead!" yelled Henri Jaspers over the phone.

"Who's Paul de Man?" I said.

"They've linked him to the Nazis during World War II!" said Henri. "Now they'll blame everything on us Deconstructionists!"

"Watch who you're calling *us*," I said.

"Communism, cult murders, the decay of the West, everything!"

"Nothing will happen, Henri," I said. "No one knows or cares about Deconstruction. I should, but I don't."

"You know more about it than you let on," said Henri.

"It's just ideas Henri," I said. "Not the kind of thing you give your life for. Would you give your life for Deconstruction, Henri?"

"Don't be funny," Henri said. "Derrida himself has received several death threats this year."

"We should blame somebody, don't you think?" said my wife, Gala, when I got off the phone. "We can't blame the powerful or the rich. Let's give the poor a break for a while and blame the intellectuals."

"For what?" I said. "It's all just something to kick around. A way for people to spend their time."

"Intellectuality?" said Gala, "or persecution?"

I am always wrong to ignore Gala, though it does not stop me. Once again, far ahead of me, she knew the beginning of a sad story.

Henri Jaspers wasn't French or German. He was from Eagle Pass, a Texas border town just across the Rio Grande from Piedras Negras in the state of Coahuila, Mexico, where both his parents, Marie and Autor Desconocido, were born and raised. They gave all six of their children European first and second names so that later in life, if they chose, they could drop their Mexican surname. Something Henri did.

As a child Henri traveled around the southwest and California with his parents, working as a migrant farmer as the family followed the harvests of citrus, strawberries, tomatoes and almonds from winter to fall. Of the six children, three—two brothers and a sister—died in a freak, summer flash flood that raged through an arroyo outside Phoenix, where the family had camped with other migrant families. Henri had a brother in Tijuana with whom he never spoke, and a sister who married a neighborhood *cholo* and moved to San Antonio.

The move across the river from Piedras Negras to Eagle Pass was the big one for Henri's family. Henri's big move was American high school, which he entered at age twenty, and then college at Southwest Texas State where he turned on to—of all things— nineteenth-century philosophy and literature, in particular Nietzsche and Conrad. That's right, Henri Jaspers Desconocido studied nihilism.

Henri couldn't get into the University of Texas for graduate school, though had he admitted on his application that he was full-blooded Mexican, and Mestizo to boot, it wouldn't have been a problem. He probably could have gone someplace like Harvard, Yale or Cal-Irvine where he, well, belonged.

By then he'd already dropped the name Desconocido so no one could tell he was Mexican, as if you couldn't tell by looking, unless you were one of those people who confused Mexicans with Japanese. No kidding, people do. I did when I first came West. But they don't ask for pictures anymore on college applications.

Later, after he got his Ph.D. from the University of Houston and became a scholar of relative renown, publishing his dissertation on Conrad, then a book on Nietzsche, and another on Wittgenstein, he still lost out on numerous academic positions to lesser scholars because he refused to "take advantage," as he said, of his heritage. He wanted to make it on his own. He ended up at the University of Utah.

That's where I met him, when Gala was hooked up to the U of U getting her M.A. Back then she was a serious poet, which she isn't anymore; in fact, she isn't even Gala anymore. She's Calamity Ray, cowgirl poet and humorist. Of course a lot of cowboy poets tell her she's not a real cowgirl, but she tells them they're not real poets.

Henri himself always thought I was a Utah native, a cowboy, and he was shocked to find out I lived my first twenty-five years in Pennsylvania. Anyway, now I am kind of a cowboy in that I do a lot of riding and shooting, but when I moved to Utah from northern California I was mostly into surfing and motorcycles.

Back in Utah, people feared Henri. He was a tyrant in the classroom and no one took his courses unless they were required to and had no other choice. Gala took his course in literary criticism while she was there, thinking she'd meet him head on, and he flunked her. Not too long after that, Henri married a famous film critic named Naomi Seidman who one day, a few months into the marriage, hanged herself from the rafters above their bed.

Something like that usually has an effect on you and in Henri's case it just made him more distant, more unapproachable. When I left Utah, Henri wasn't teaching or talking to anybody at all. He got a grant and left for France to research his next book on the founder of Deconstruction, Jacques Derrida.

I guess when Henri came back to Salt Lake City, that's when he met his current wife, a beautiful, blonde, Jack-Mormon princess named Jarri who worked as a secretary in the Department of English until Henri whisked her off her feet.

I heard reports that Jarri attended all of Henri's classes and recorded his lectures. Henri, his long, black hair twisted into a tight braid that ran down his back, liked to goose-step around the classroom and never took questions; he thought it gave him an air of, well, authority, for lack of a better word. Henri himself said that he was a Fascist in the classroom. Soon Jarri became pregnant, and then a mother, and then a pregnant mother, and then a mother of two, and then very depressed and so spent five days a week with a Freudian shrink with whom she naturally fell in love. Henri could understand that, being an intellectual. It was simply a matter of transference.

That's where things stood when, soon after Henri's phone call to me, just after Paul de Man's death, Henri and Jarri made their trip to L.A. Henri had studied with Derrida in France and had made an appointment to meet him in Irvine for lunch. Derrida taught down there now part of the year. Seeing as me and Henri were old friends, he and Jarri and the kids came to our place to stay.

For Jarri, the trip to Los Angeles was very traumatic because she didn't like to be away from her shrink for so long. It made her very insecure about everything, especially her looks, and after sleeping in until eleven she spent several hours in the bathroom, emerging looking much the same as she did when she went in (though Gala assured me that it was a highly manicured natural look, and Jarri herself admitted she could go nowhere without her Chanel lipstick).

Both of their kids were delightful and played wonderfully with my daughter, though Jarri paid no attention to them at all. Henri, a man transformed by fatherhood, ran around our house cooing, "Oh, what do you need my little sweeties? Ah, baby want ooh-aahh-ooh-goo," and fetched them everything.

"Let's go see Madonna tonight," said Jarri as she came out of the bathroom.

"Derrida's speaking at UCLA," said Henri.

"Madonna tickets could be tough," I said.

"At this short notice," said Gala who, to be honest, regarded Madonna as a reactionary.

Of course Henri loved Madonna in that way that a lot of intellectuals did, indulging his prurient interests by rationalizing her sexuality into some kind of role-reversal thing. He and Gala were done arguing about it and they'd reduced the vendetta to aphorism.

"She's a reverse paradigm," said Henri.

"Sex is sex. Analysis is paralysis," said Gala.

"She stole that from me," I said to Henri.

"In the postmodern era, authorship is an anachronism," said Henri.

"Do you tell that to your students who plagiarize?" said Gala.

I flipped a quarter. "Heads Madonna, tails Derrida," I said.

"Shouldn't that be heads Derrida, tails Madonna? Or are you attempting to subvert the obvious mind-body pun and dualism?" said Gala.

"Not intentionally," I said. "It's tails."

"You see? The coin flip is a text! We can argue about its meaning!" yelled Henri.

"Calm down, Henri," I said.

"Well, at least we'll get in to see Derrida," said Jarri.

"You think so," said Henri.

"Henri," said Gala, "this is LA. No one has even heard of Derrida."

"He's teaching over at Irvine, right Henri?" I said. "Anybody can see him whenever they want. Aren't you having lunch with him tomorrow?"

"He's a lot like Carlos Castenada," said Henri. "Do you understand the metaphor?"

"Like Castenada," said Gala, "Derrida can't be found, even when he's present."

"Let's get a baby-sitter and get going," said Jarri.

So we called our baby-sitter and packed into the van, heading north out of the canyon to the Ventura Freeway, then down the San Diego Freeway to Sunset Boulevard and Westwood. We arrived at UCLA an hour and a half early and the place was already packed, an auditorium of three thousand seats jammed full, people spilling out into the crammed vestibule and onto the steps.

"Jesus," said Gala.

"I told you," Henri said irritably.

I fipped a quarter. "Heads Madonna, tails Derrida," I said.

A young man pushed by me murmuring, "I lost my keys in there. I lost my car keys and there's an emergency," but he was stopped cold a few feet ahead of me and thrown to the back.

Then a woman behind us screamed, "Please, let me through, I left my baby in there!" The crowd turned on her viciously. She pushed forward, pleading, and Henri put an elbow in her face.

There was a surge and the crowd pushed against the doors, screams rising from the front.

"Stop this!" I yelled. I raised my arms. "Stop this! We're all here to see Derrida! I'm sure if we send an emissary to the front they'll find a way to let us in!"

"A trick!" someone yelled.

"No!" I said. "No! Here, send Henri Jaspers! He knows Derrida!"

Remarkably, another man there had heard of Henri and in no time we'd pushed Henri forward. From outside the building we could hear him pleading into the back of the auditorium, and then someone else emerged and said if we were orderly we could come in and sit in the aisles or even on stage.

A cheer arose from the crowd. The excitement and calm with which people filed into the crowded place was amazing. I'll tell you, it brought tears to my eyes the way that place filled, the aisles a sea of sentience, the stage itself a mass of bodies. I could not find Henri, but Jarri, Gala and I ended up at the foot of the stage, right below the podium.

When Derrida himself emerged we were crushed by the silence of awe as the bodies on the stage parted like a wheat field. I saw him, briefly, as he approached the microphone, a short, dapper man with neat, cropped, gray hair. But once he placed himself at the podium, all I could see was the tip of a single loafer. His foot appeared small and Gala reminded us that he played soccer as a boy in Algeria during the World War II.

Outside the auditorium, the crowd again had doubled and pressed itself viscerally against the auditorium walls. I hadn't felt such massive claustrophobia since I'd been in the subway at rush hour in Mexico City, and couldn't help but think of the disastrous consequences if someone should panic, or if there was a fire.

Derrida began his paper on the proto-Marxist critic Walter Benjamin, dedicating the reading to his friend, the departed Paul de Man. The audience, by the thousands, oozed audibly.

"It's the deadly existential contradiction of the metaphor," Gala informed me, settling her head into my lap and her feet onto the legs of a strange, balding man in wire rims and a corduroy jacket.

After two hours, in a speech overwhelming in its intellectual allusions and peppered throughout with paragraphs in French and German, Derrida announced that he was almost halfway through. The crowd, in anticipation, hissed loud enough to almost awaken Gala, who'd fallen asleep in my lap.

"Do you understand any of this?" Jarri asked me.

"Of course not," I said. "After it's over we'll find your husband and ask him."

But it was then that a man leapt up from the middle of the tenth row, as if he had finally heard the conclusive utterance of indictment; who knows, maybe he had. The crowd seemed to part from him, and his white shirt, open at the chest, billowed in the hot air. He pointed a revolver at the stage.

The crowd swayed like a huge wave and the moment froze like the execution painting by Goya.

"Deconstruction is Fascism! Derrida, you are a Nazi pig!" the man yelled.

By now, everything seemed to fall away from the corridor of lethal intent between the man and Derrida. Oddly, the gunman seethed with fear and sweat, while Derrida stared at him, his eyes calm and questioning.

"During the War I was only a boy," murmured Derrida in English, "playing soccer in the dirt streets of Algeria."

Then the man fired. Once, then again.

That's when Henri appeared, throwing himself in front of the podium. He took a bullet in the shoulder and spun against the microphone stand, clinging to it momentarily, his eyes meeting Derrida's before the apparatus collapsed under him with another bang.

The crowd seemed to rise in unison to overwhelm the gunman. The most remarkable thing about all of it was the orderliness of that huge throng. They held the man and waited for the security guards, and finally the police carted the screaming man away. His screams were the only noise, as if *he* had been shot and not Henri, who lay bleeding on the stage.

Quietly, the crowd ushered itself out, back rows first, like a great, long sigh of relief, while Derrida was pulled from the stage and rushed out the back.

Jarri held Henri's head, which I could see had been grazed by the second bullet. His wounded shoulder still poured blood in spurting rhythm with his heart. His blood covered his torso, and Jarri. Henri looked up, dazed, as if he were not quite in the moment, as if for him everything was now both different and deferred.

"You saved him," I said.

Henri blinked twice and then passed out.

Across Los Angeles, at the Hollywood Bowl, Madonna appeared to an unfilled stadium, scalpers selling tickets at half-price outside the parking lot, while here in yet another heart of Tinsel Town, in front of thousands, the son of Mexican immigrants lay bleeding, having thrown himself in front of bullets to save the life of Jacques Derrida.

The next day, while waiting to hear from Jarri, I attended an early morning workshop on bareback bronco riding in Orange County, then stopped at a McDonalds in Irvine on the way home for some French fries and coffee. There, alone in the corner of the Micky Ds, eating a hamburger, sat Derrida.

I felt like I knew him.

"I attended your lecture last night at UCLA," I said to him. "But my German isn't so good," I said. "I came with Henri."

"I was supposed to meet him for lunch today," he said.

"Yes," I said, "I know."

"It is too bad," he said. "The shot was very high. Had he kept his seat, I don't think the bullet would have hit anyone."

"I think it was instinctual on Henri's part," I said.

"Yes," said Derrida, "but even so, now it is absolutely impossible to say the bullet was intended for me."

"There certainly weren't any crowds at the McDonalds," I said later that evening to Gala.

"Like Castenada, he's probably only visible to true believers," Gala said. "Would you like a bourbon?"

"Yes, I would. Did Jarri call? I suppose we should get over to Kaiser and see Henri tomorrow."

"Absolutely," said Gala. "Just do me a favor and remember this isn't a short story, Harlan. It's not a story, so don't write it down. Don't write about it."

I took the bourbon on the rocks from her and had a hot sip. "Of course not," I said.

M E I N   K A M P F

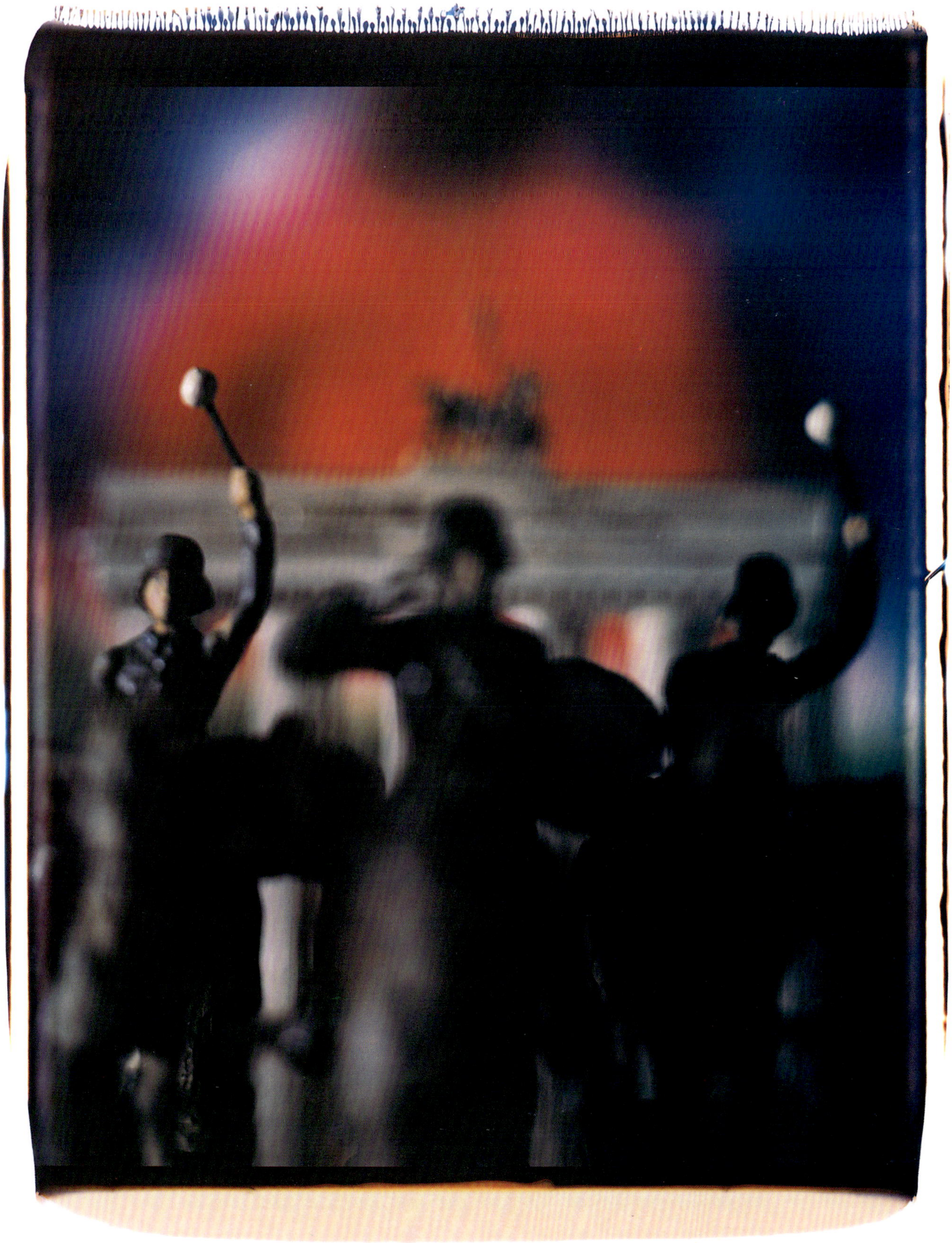

DAVID LEVINTHAL

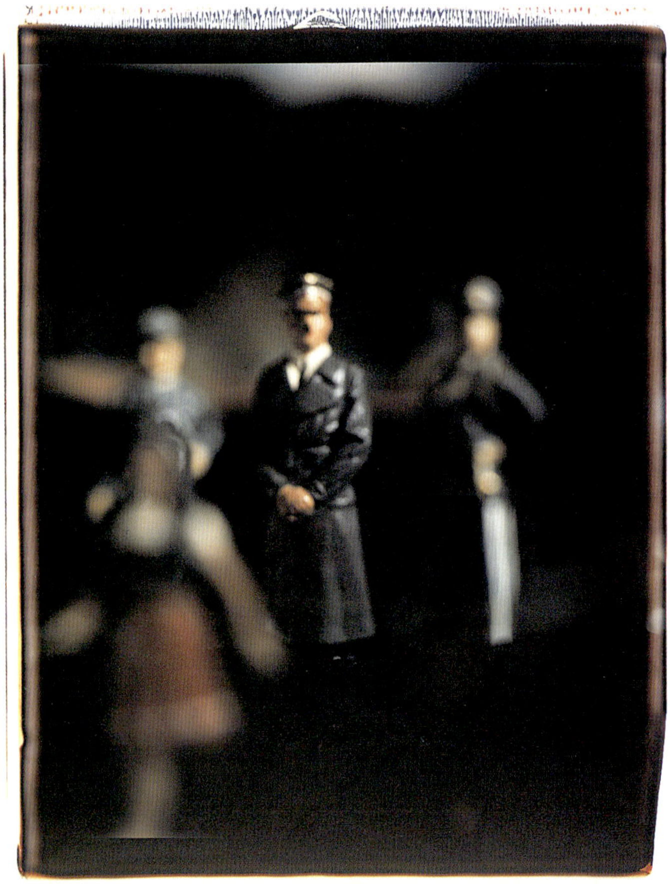

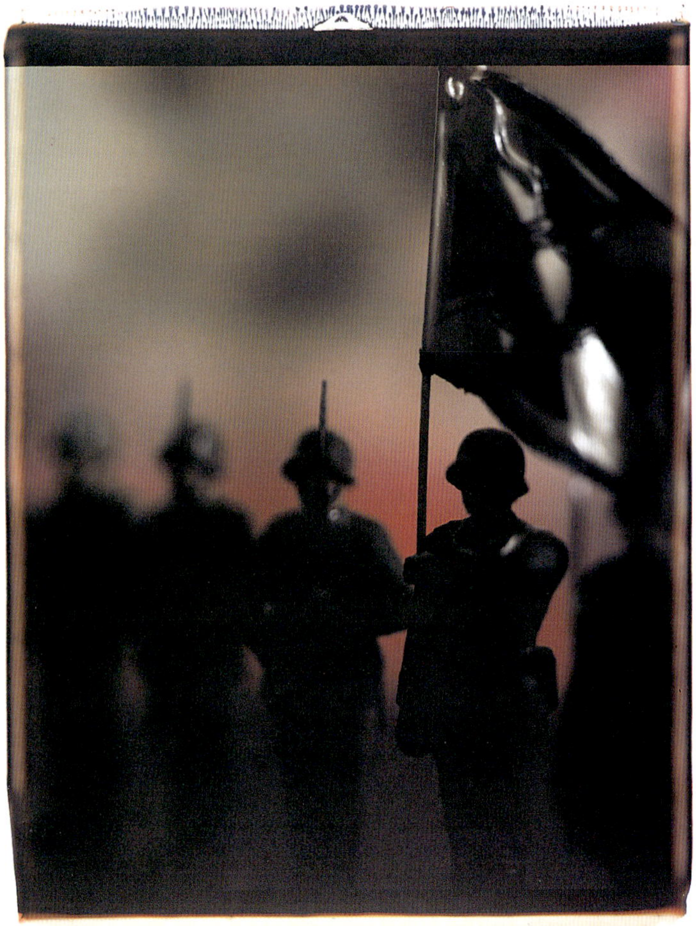

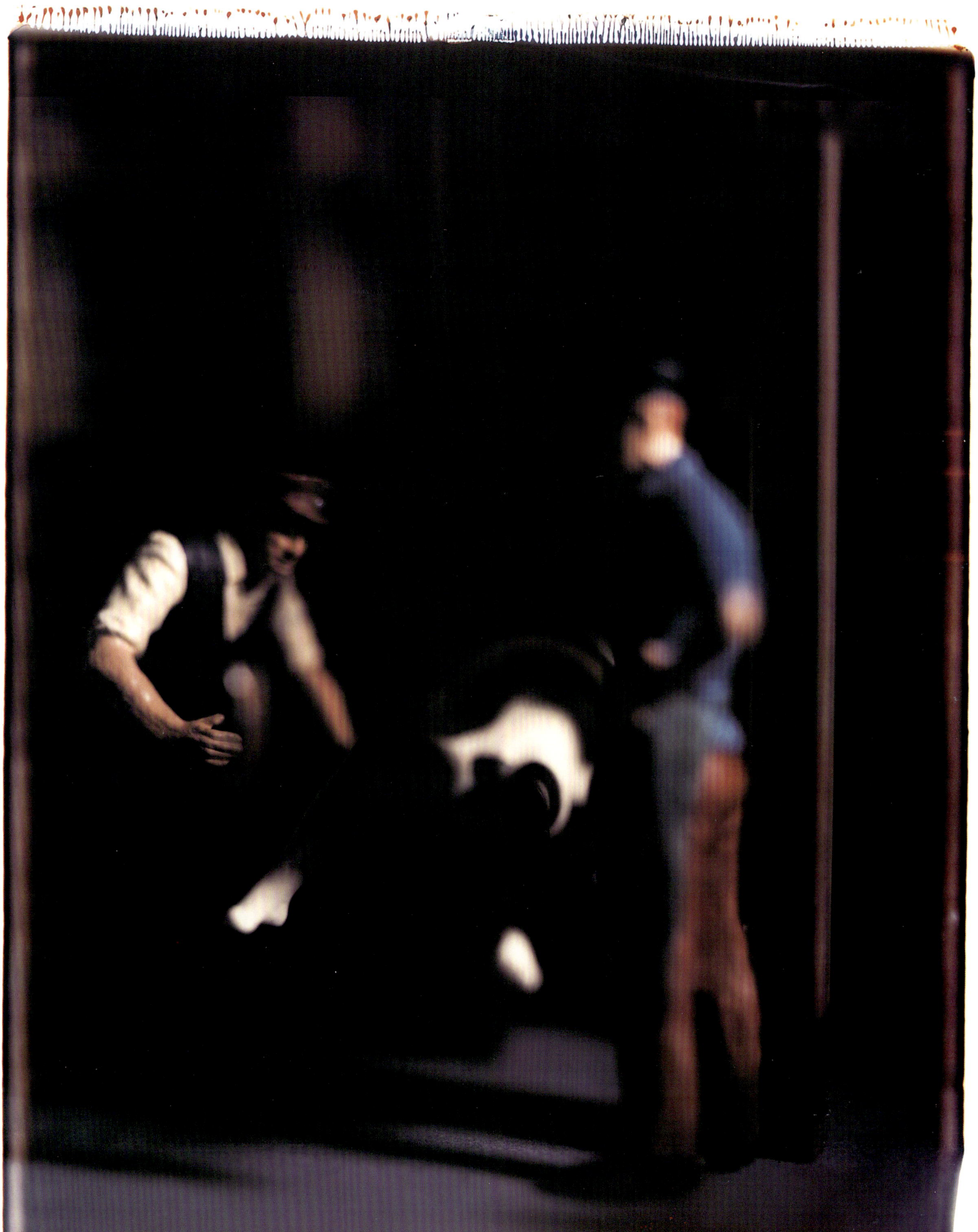

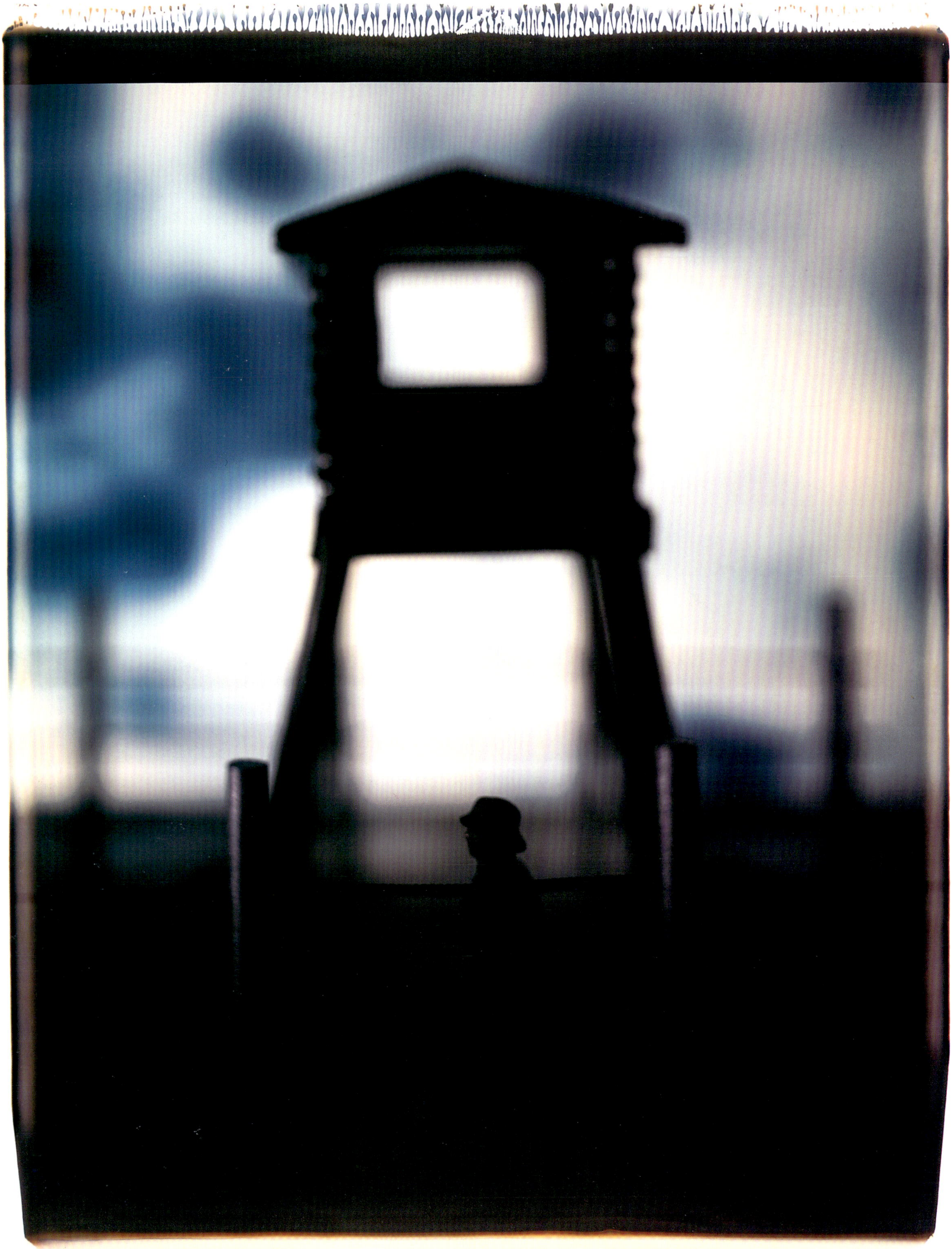

TOYING WITH HISTORY

A CONVERSATION WITH DAVID LEVINTHAL, WILLIAM CHRISTENBERRY AND MERRY FORESTA

PHOTOGRAPHS THAT DEPICT REAL EVENTS in real time are often powerful and disturbing, but what do we make of pictures that refer to powerful and disturbing events in metaphoric, artistically oblique ways? For more than twenty years, David Levinthal and William Christenberry have utilized toy figures to examine, in a blur of emotional ambiguity and half-remembered history, the dreams and extremes of a decidedly adult world.

Although they had never met before, we asked them to sit down with Merry Foresta, Curator of Photography at the National Museum of American Art, Smithsonian Institution, to discuss their shared methods and shared urge to manfacture images of unspeakable terrors. They met in Christenberry's studio in Washington, D.C.

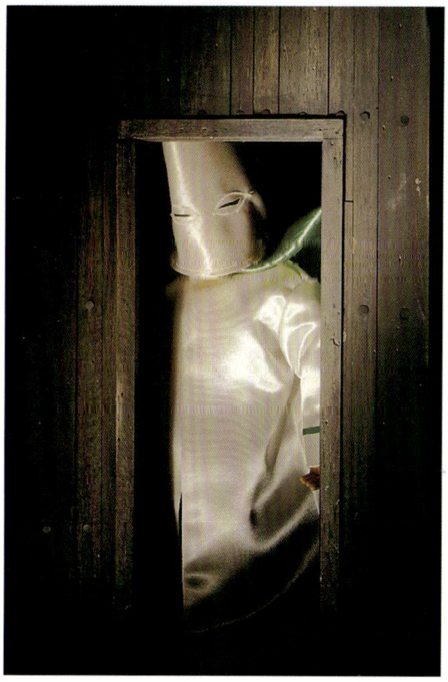

William Christenberry, from *The Klan Room*, 1982.

MERRY FORESTA: THIS CONVERSATION IS TAKING PLACE AT AN APPROPRIATE TIME, with the fiftieth anniversary of the end of World War II and the liberation of Auschwitz. We're also witnessing the continuing rise of neo-Nazism in parts of Europe, and racism still is thriving throughout the United States. In your work, you both raise difficult questions surrounding our century's violent history and the ways it is perceived by the public and pictured by artists. I'd like to talk about the choices you've made to explore this history using toys and dolls, and to discuss the mysteries that infuse your works dealing with the Holocaust and Ku Klux Klan.

David, in the past you've used toys to set up and stick pins in American myths, as in the cowboys and Indians photographs and the sexually charged *Desire* series. In the '70s, you began to re-create World War II scenes with toys for the *Hitler Moves East* project. How did you make the transition from that work to the *Mein Kampf* images?

DAVID LEVINTHAL: I tend to be very object-oriented in my work. I began this series after finding a contemporary Hitler figurine in Austria. I discovered that there was a man in Germany who had molds from the '30s and who was remaking these figures and hand-painting them. I remember seeing some similar toys back in the '70s when I was doing the *Hitler Moves East* book, but they didn't interest me at the time because I wasn't looking for the specificity of Hitler. That book was really more about the fabrication of reality, while the *Mein Kampf* series deals with the symbolism and iconography of the Nazis. I've called the series *Mein Kampf* because it encompasses both the vision of the Holocaust and the pageantry of the Nazis.

My initial idea was to try to do some August Sander-like portraits of these little figures. I envisioned a small series of maybe twenty images. That was the starting point. I remember shooting a Hitler figure and not being happy with it. The image either was too soft or it revealed too much detail in the toys, such as cracks in the face mold.

MF: How did the series evolve beyond these first attempts?

DL: My general way of working is to do visual research. Before I even had a title for this series, I was watching Leni Riefenstahl's Nazi propaganda film, *Triumph of the Will.* I was so taken by the power of those images. The portraits weren't working, so I decided to try some images inspired by the film. I grouped together a number of figures to resemble a parade, and I set up a railroad archway and had Hitler walking through it, saluting. I also changed my palate to red and silver and black. It's a very militaristic color scheme.

The more visual material I found, particularly old film footage on television and videotape, the more I understood that the pageantry of the Nazis was a vital element of their power. An incredible sense of nationalism emerged from those rallies. It was not by accident that many of the rallies were held at night; the torchlit parades achieved extra dramatic effect.

WILLIAM CHRISTENBERRY: Exactly. Your pictures remind me of the pageantry that's so much a part of the Klan. The secret night meetings, the cross burnings...

DL: Pageantry is a big part of militarism, whether it's Nazis or Klansmen, Communists or Americans. Look at Frank Capra's *Why We Fight* series, which I remember seeing in junior high school. It's very stirring. *Triumph of the Will* has a similar effect. When you watch it you want to sign up.

WC: Same with the Klan rally I attended in Alabama in the summer of '66. I could understand why some people would join. Before I actually attended a rally, I always envisioned the cross being maybe eight feet high, but I saw two telephone poles put up by a crane, wrapped in burlap bags and soaked in gasoline and oil. I'll never forget the sound when they lit it. Then, almost as if it had been choreographed, a big Alabama harvest moon

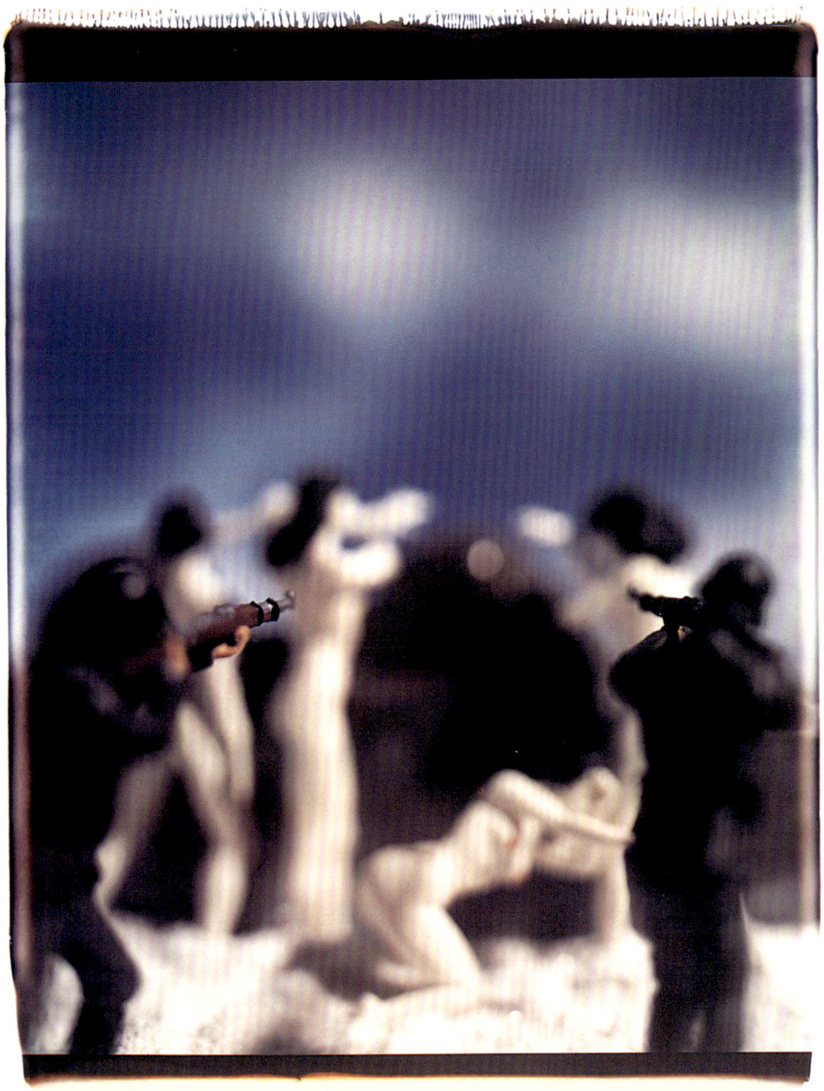

David Levinthal, from *Mein Kampf*, 1994.

rose in the distance. I swear you could feel the fervor of those people.

MF: There is this conflict in the pageantry—and in both of your depictions of it—between the awesome and the horrific, the beautiful and the repulsive. Were you drawn to these contradictions, David, while you assembled your imagery?

DL: There was a particular image that I kept seeing, while looking at documentary photographs from the war, of a group of nude women running across a field towards a gas chamber. It's shot at an angle and obviously taken surreptitiously by one of the German guards. The image was so powerful, and I wanted to try an interpretation of it. I used some of my miniature Japanese doll figures that I had gotten for the *Desire* series. I set three of them up against a barbed-wire background made from silver elasticized bands that usually are used as Christmas decorations. I placed two SS figures in the foreground and shot the image over their shoulders. I used plumes of red paint to capture a sense of fire. In a lot of the reading I did, people talk about the sky glowing red when they walked around the camps at night. These colors and the lack of depth of field, which is my signature style, created this very eerie, almost operatic Holocaust scene.

When that image came out of the Polaroid camera I was really overwhelmed. As a viewer, you become one of the guards because of your vantage point. You become a participant.

MF: Exactly. I thought of Goya's *Assassination of Maximilian* because of the over-the-shoulder perspective both in his painting and your photograph. You raise difficult questions of identity and indictment. Viewers have to question whether or not they would be holding that gun. It's similar to looking at some of the Klan doll photographs, in which we're put in the position of being seduced by the shapes, the beautiful fabrics and the rally scene. Have either of you thought of Goya as an influence?

WC: Actually, Goya is of critical importance to me. One of my images is an homage to him. It depicts a Klansman doll dressed all in white with red trim; he's hooded, of course. He's in a glass-front house that is painted black. He's sleeping on an American flag pillow, and right underneath his neck is a smaller Confederate flag pillow, because the Klan abuses both the American flag and the Confederate flag. It's outright homage to Goya's allegory: the sleep of reason produces monsters.

DL: When I first showed the image of the SS guards facing the three women, one viewer said to me, "This is very Goya-like." I hadn't thought of it before, but the image does have that dark and moody quality.

MF: The entire series is very evocative of that foreboding mood.

DL: For me, the signature image in the series is the guard tower; it's also a good example of how my images come into being. I was in Poland last summer and I visited the camps at Auschwitz and Buchenwald. Of all my visual memories of this trip, the most powerful is standing alone in the tower at Buchenwald, looking out over the camp's 440 acres. Looking down, you get that sense of distance and power that the guards must have felt. The view dehumanizes the individuals below.

I had a funny feeling when I was in Auschwitz. It's a relatively small town, and its biggest industry probably is tourism. I thought it must be very odd to be a Pole living in this city. The analogy I came up with was if you were living in a small southern town and there was a tree on which a number of people had been lynched, and people came to see it.

MF: They're both monuments to something horrible, as are the photographs that you both create. Are either of you worried about how people may interpret these images?

WC: Some people have misconstrued the Klan dolls. Some of the comments I've read about my work in museum guest books are really hurtful. One person wrote, "Thank god for New York. I hate Alabama." Someone else wrote, "William Christenberry's Klan tableaux glorifies and beautifies the Ku Klux Klan." I also remember another comment: "You nigger-lovers can stick it." Of course, many people have been complimentary. The work illicits all of these different responses.

DL: I'm aware that some people may respond in a superficial way. Still, I think most people see the horrific side, also.

MF: There is a certain purgative quality to the work for many viewers, and I imagine for both of you as well.

DL: I think for me there is. This was a really tough series. Subconsciously, there's a self-purging going on. This is something that I should be caring about and involved with, first as a human being and then as a Jew. But I wasn't approaching this work thinking, I'm a Jew and I'm going to do something about the Holocaust. The creative process really slows to a halt if I analyze what the work means. I push those intellectual and critical thoughts away when I'm working, and concentrate on striving for a particular atmosphere.

I don't know how you work, Bill, but when I get involved in a project I go at it with blinders on. Several people commented to me, when I'd show them work in progress, "How do you live with this work? Don't you get upset?" The images don't really affect me that way, because while I'm working I think more in terms of problem-solving.

MF: What about you, Bill? Is the creation of these images a form of catharsis?

WC: I often wonder about that. Maybe it does give me some relief, at least when I'm working on it. Ed Kienholz visited my studio once and told me, "This is your obsession. You just continue to deal with it as hard as you can." Sometimes I look at this body of work and wonder, did I create this? I'm still trying to come to grips with it, and probably will for the rest of my life.

I do feel that it's significant that someone of my background chose to deal with the Klan as subject matter. I used to think that I was a pure white Southerner, but I found out that my grandmother had Cherokee blood in her. I will say something here that I used to think but never said out loud: I feel certain that if I were non-white, I wouldn't have had any problems getting the Klan work exhibited or seen. The fact that I'm a Southerner also has inhibited it to some degree.

MF: Well, you're suspect for both of those reasons.

WC: See, I started this as private work, as a response to my feelings about the Klan. But there always will be people who say that David and I are wrong, that we have no right to deal with this subject matter.

DL: Or that we're trivializing this subject matter.

WC: I'm no writer, but I want to read you one short paragraph that I wrote several years ago about my work: "Some people have told me that this subject is not the proper concern of an artist or of art. On the contrary, I hold the position that there are times when an artist must examine and reveal such strange and secret brutality."

MF: Do you have a sense of responsibility about handling this kind of material?

DL: I think that both of us are responsible people in general. I don't think there's anything exploitative about what Bill's doing or what I'm doing. We're drawn to these subjects. I'm very aware that I'm dealing with an extremely sensitive subject, more so than with any other work I've done in the past.

My view is that Bill and I are opening up a dialogue about these issues, and if we're responsible in the way we present our ideas, then there's nothing wrong with the questions and responses they generate.

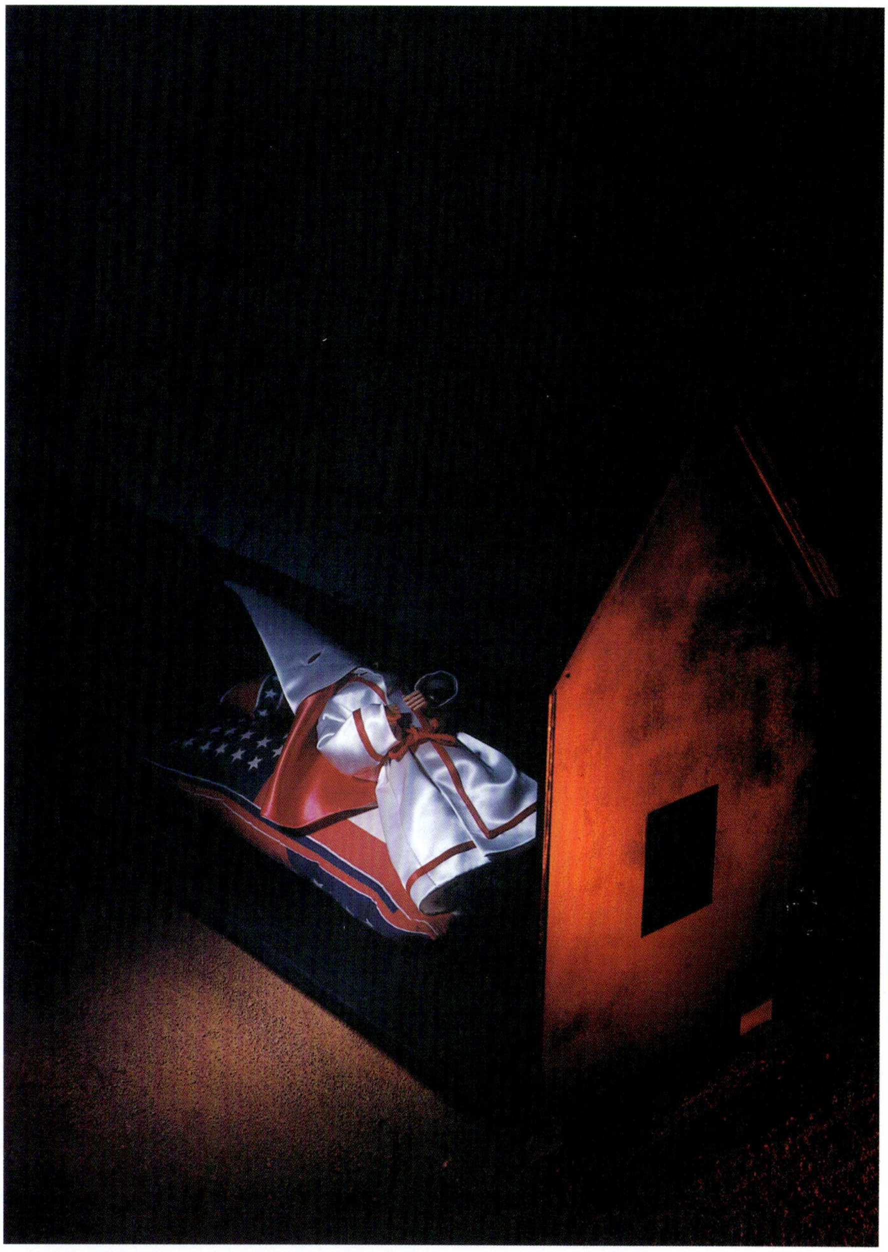

William Christenberry, from *The Klan Room,* 1982.

To tell how forms changed to new bodies:

you gods changed them, so breathe

on my efforts & keep this poem, from creation

to my own time, coming!

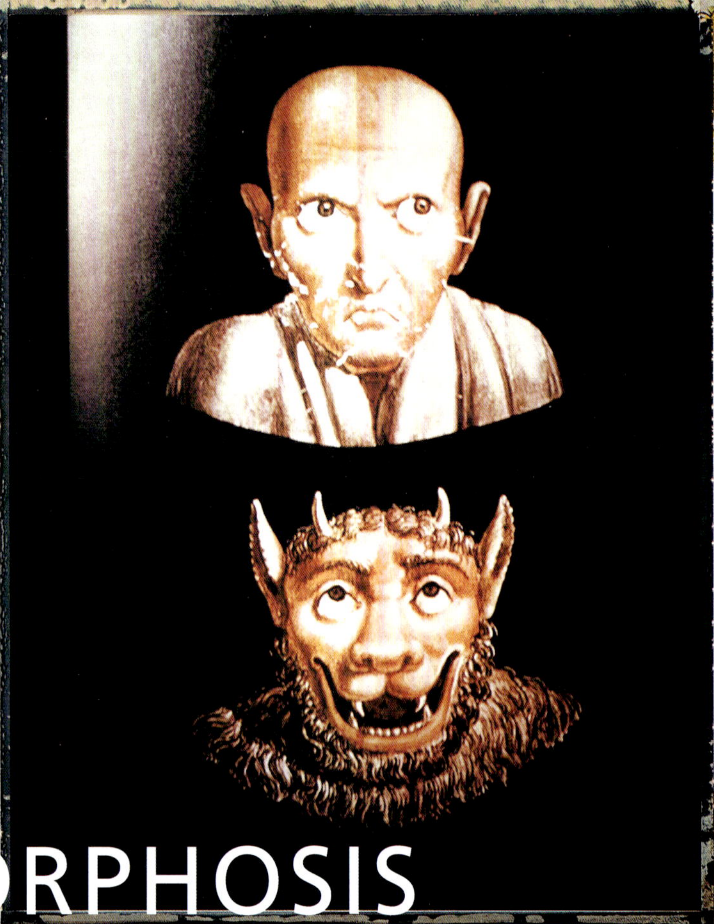

RICK HOCK

METAMORPHOSIS

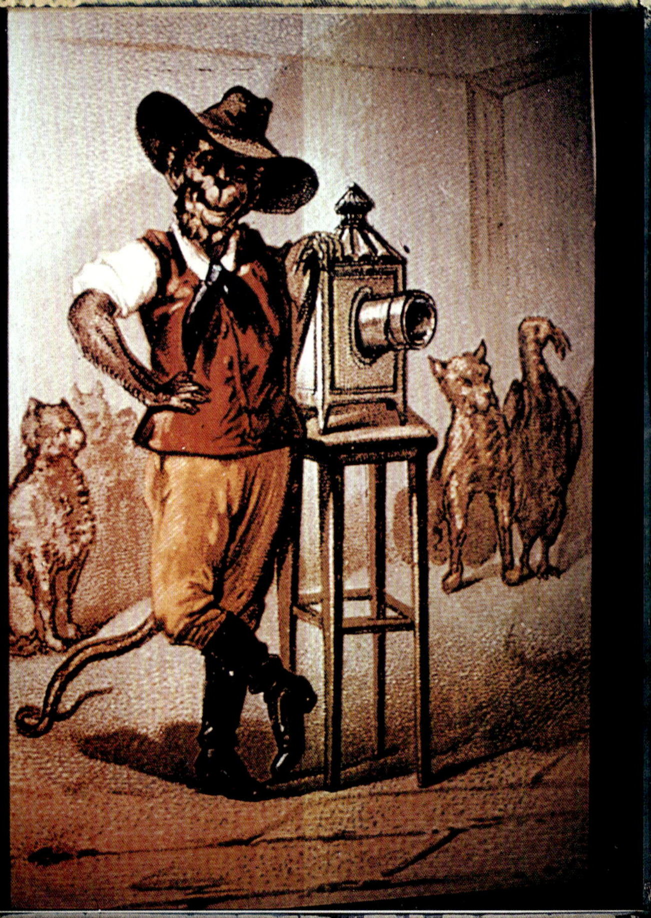

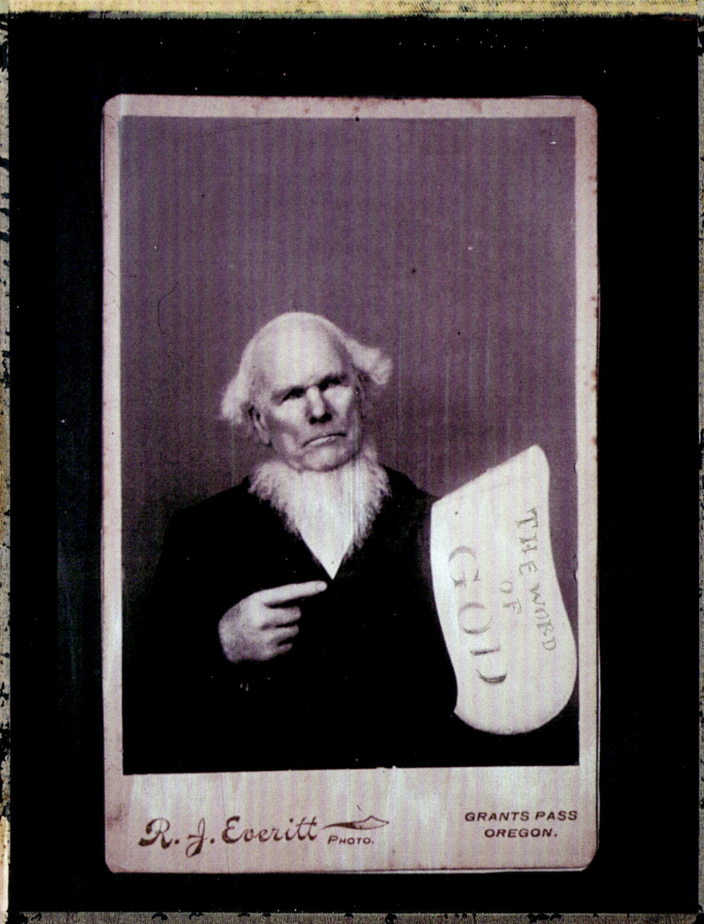

OPEN SPACE, a regular feature of see, provides a blank canvas for artists involved with the photo novella, image/text works and other means of presentation that defy classification. Each project is conceived specifically for these pages; participating artists are confined only by the size and shape of the journal. For this issue these pages belong to Rick Hock.

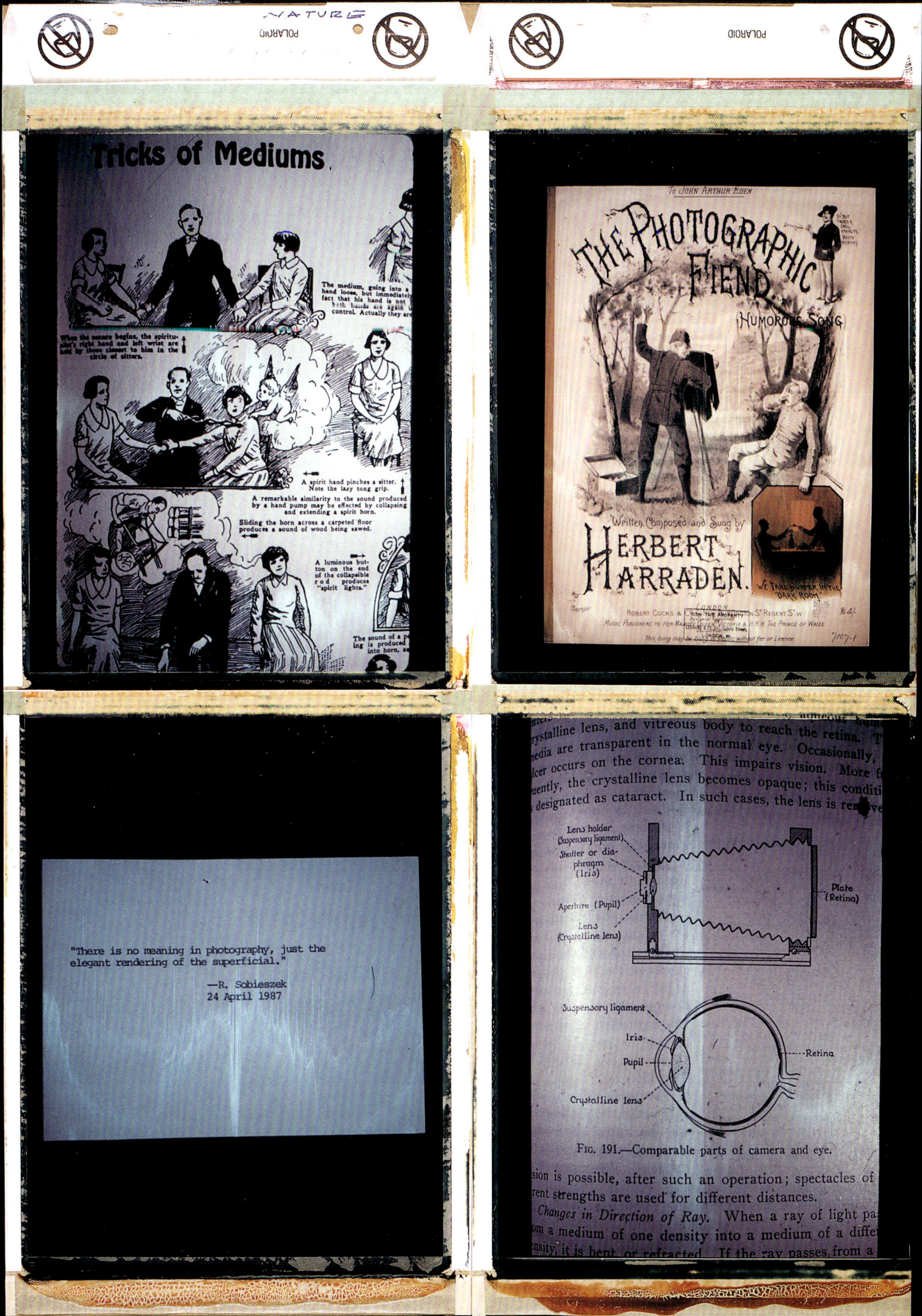
NATURE
POLAROID
POLAROID
Tricks of Mediums
The medium, going into a hand loose, but immediately fact that his hand is not both hands are again control. Actually they are
When the seance begins, the spiritualist's right hand and left wrist are held by those closest to him in the circle of sitters.
A spirit hand pinches a sitter. Note the lazy tong grip.
A remarkable similarity to the sound produced by a hand pump may be effected by collapsing and extending a spirit horn.
Sliding the horn across a carpeted floor produces a sound of wood being sawed.
A luminous button on the end of the collapsible rod produces "spirit lights."
The sound of a p ing is produced into horn, a
To John Arthur Eden
The Photographic Fiend.
(Humorous Song)
Written, Composed and Sung by
Herbert Harraden.
We take supper in the "Dark Room"
LONDON
Robert Cocks & Co.
Music Publishers to Her Majesty Queen Victoria & H.R.H. The Prince of Wales
"There is no meaning in photography, just the elegant rendering of the superficial."
—R. Sobieszek
24 April 1987
rystalline lens, and vitreous body to reach the retina. T
edia are transparent in the normal eye. Occasionally,
lcer occurs on the cornea. This impairs vision. More f
uently, the crystalline lens becomes opaque; this conditi
designated as cataract. In such cases, the lens is re ve
Lens holder (Suspensory ligament)
Shutter or diaphragm (Iris)
Aperture (Pupil)
Lens (Crystalline lens)
Plate (Retina)
Suspensory ligament
Iris
Pupil
Crystalline lens
Retina
Fig. 191.—Comparable parts of camera and eye.
sion is possible, after such an operation; spectacles of
rent strengths are used for different distances.
Changes in Direction of Ray. When a ray of light pa
om a medium of one density into a medium of a diffe
nsity, it is bent, or refracted. If the ray passes from a

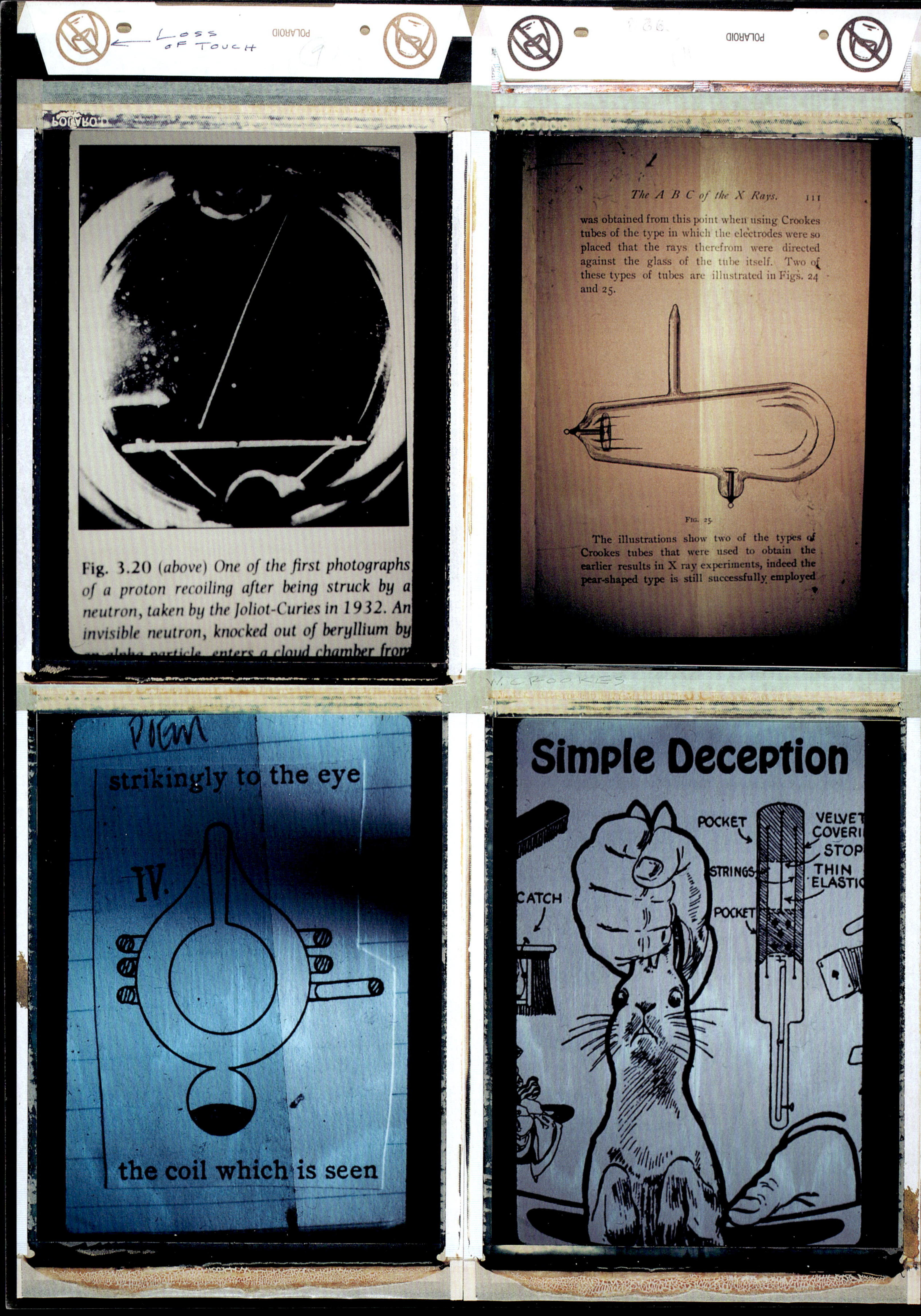
LOSS OF TOUCH
POLAROID
Fig. 3.20 (above) One of the first photographs of a proton recoiling after being struck by a neutron, taken by the Joliot-Curies in 1932. An invisible neutron, knocked out of beryllium by
The A B C of the X Rays. 111
was obtained from this point when using Crookes tubes of the type in which the electrodes were so placed that the rays therefrom were directed against the glass of the tube itself. Two of these types of tubes are illustrated in Figs. 24 and 25.
Fig. 25.
The illustrations show two of the types of Crookes tubes that were used to obtain the earlier results in X ray experiments, indeed the pear-shaped type is still successfully employed
W. CROOKES
POEM
strikingly to the eye
IV.
the coil which is seen
Simple Deception
POCKET
STRINGS
POCKET
CATCH

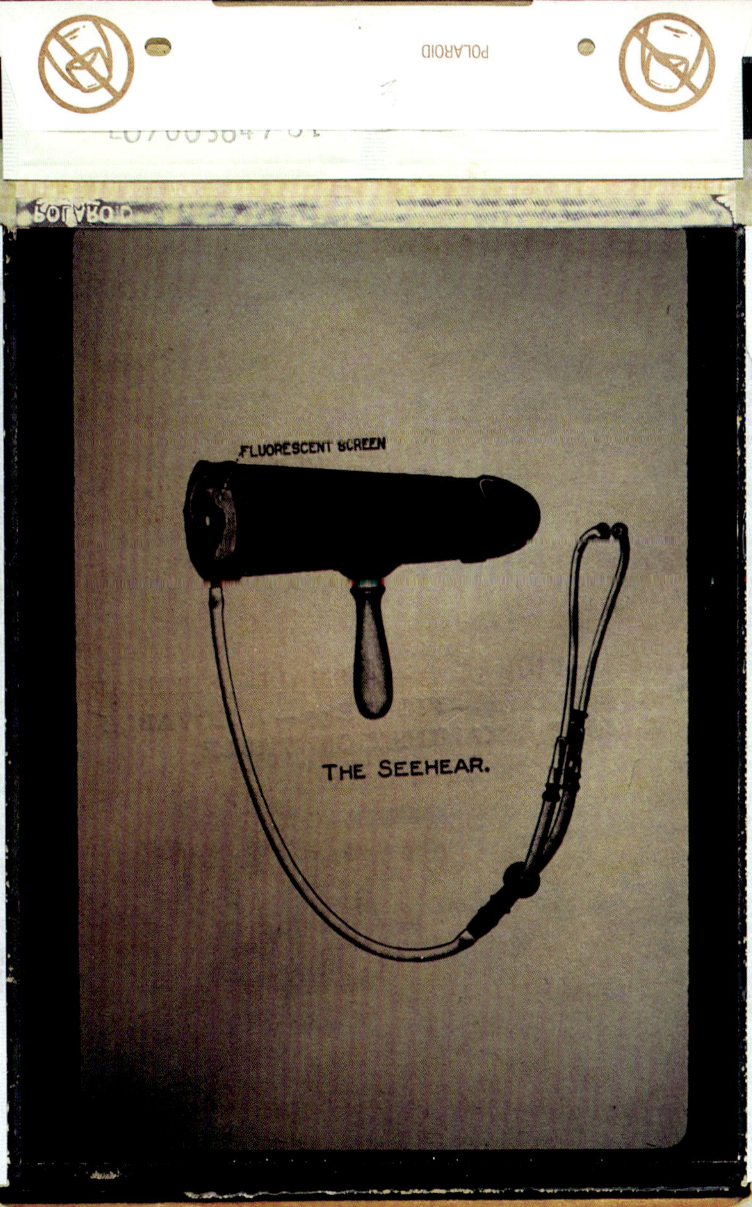
POLAROID
FLUORESCENT SCREEN
THE SEEHEAR.

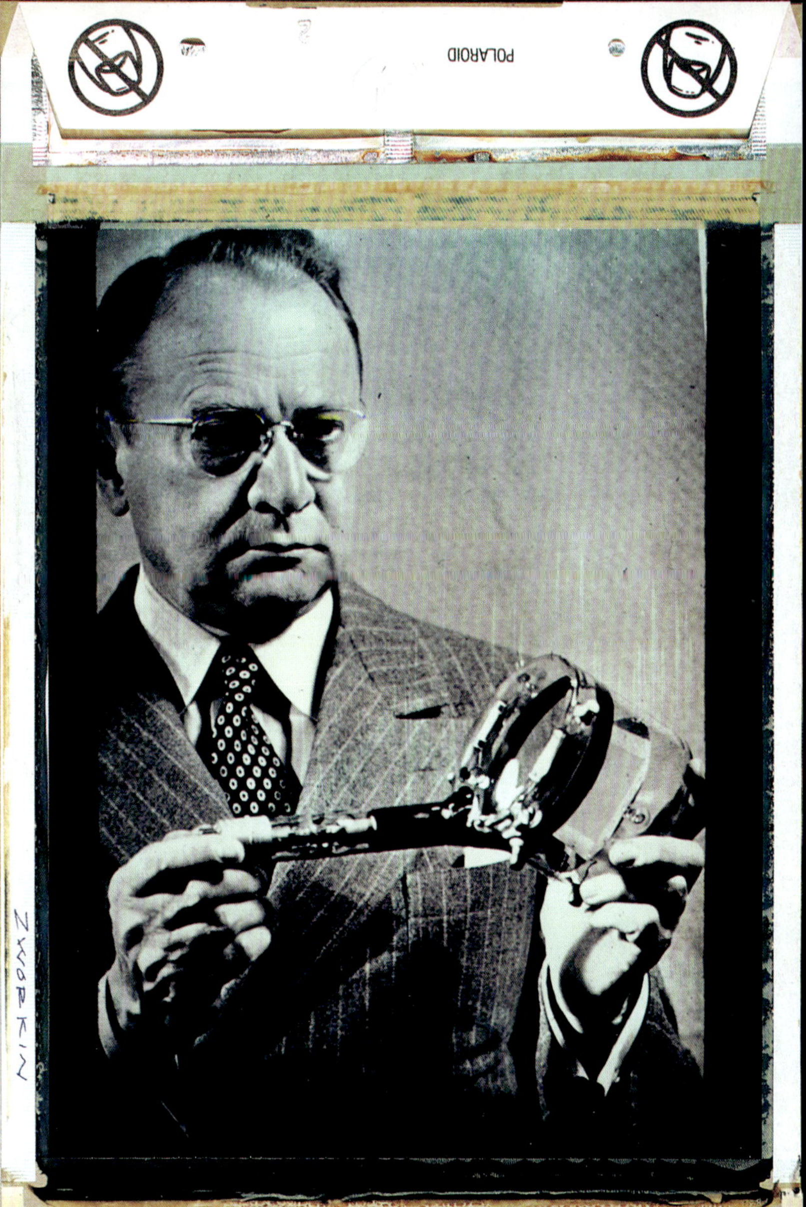
POLAROID
ZWORKIN

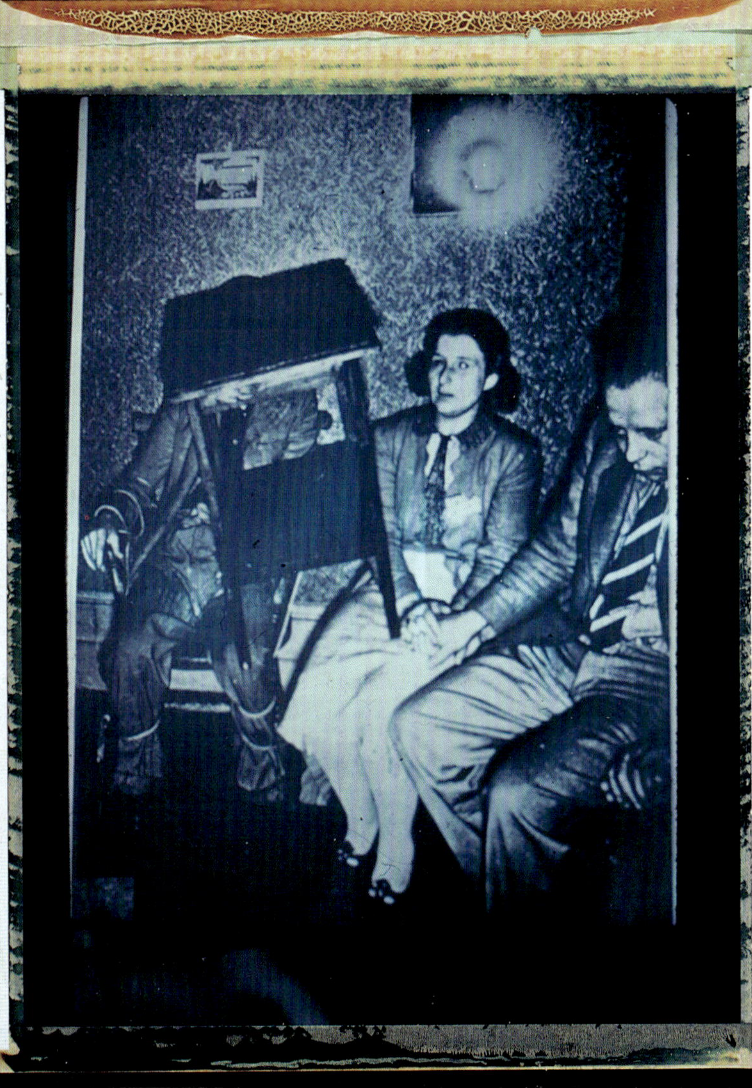

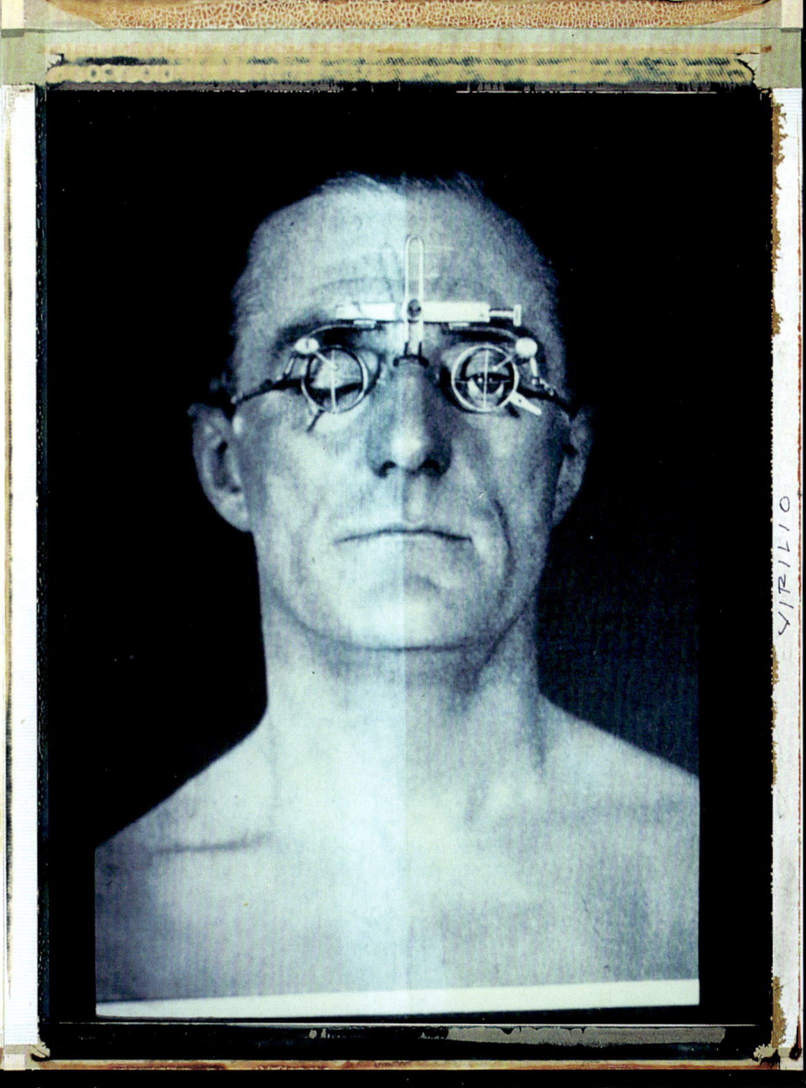
VIRILIO

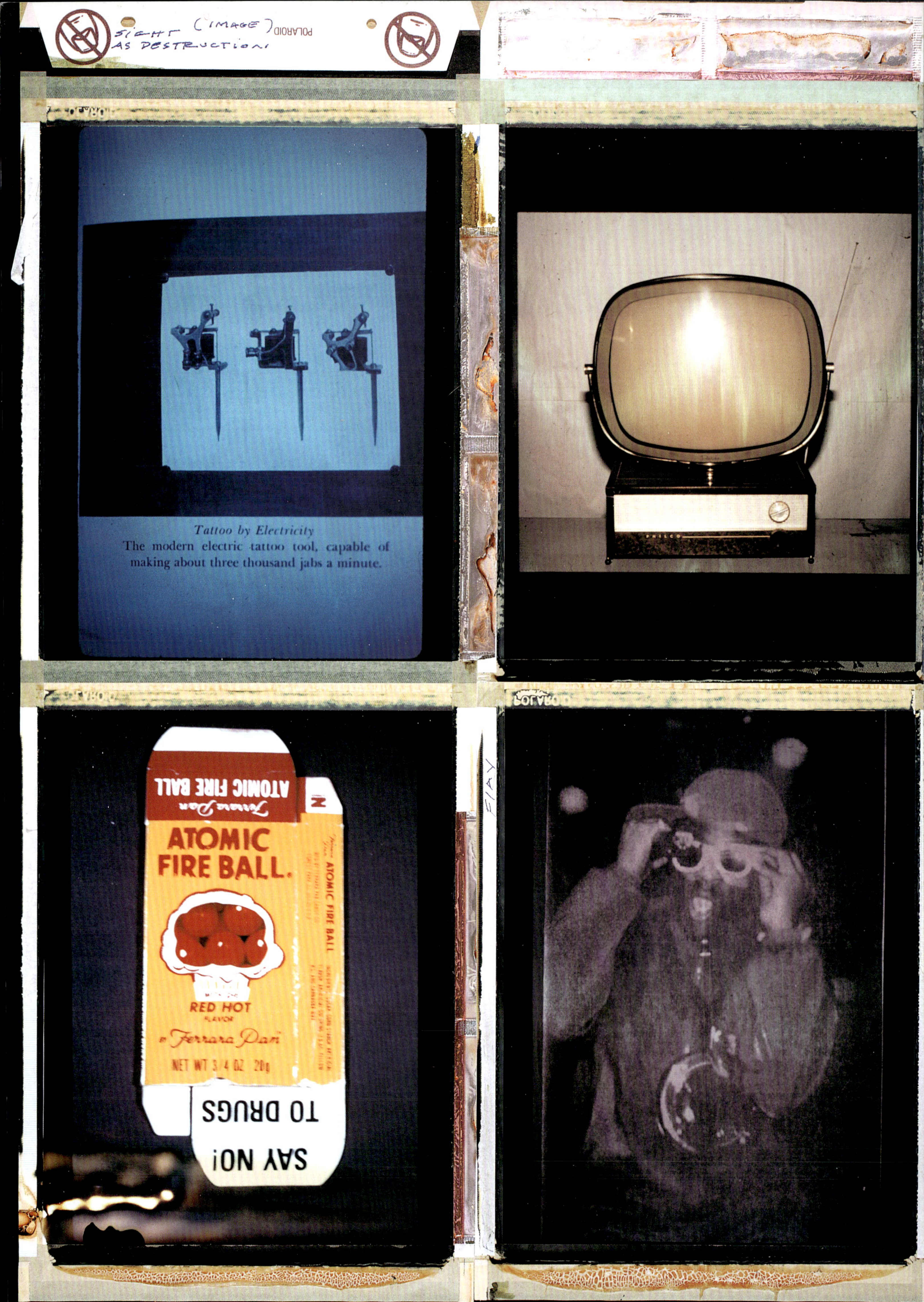

SIGHT (IMAGE) AS DESTRUCTION
POLAROID
Tattoo by Electricity
The modern electric tattoo tool, capable of making about three thousand jabs a minute.
PHILCO
ATOMIC FIRE BALL
Ferrara Pan
ATOMIC FIRE BALL.
RED HOT FLAVOR
Ferrara Pan
NET WT 3/4 OZ 20g
SAY NO! TO DRUGS

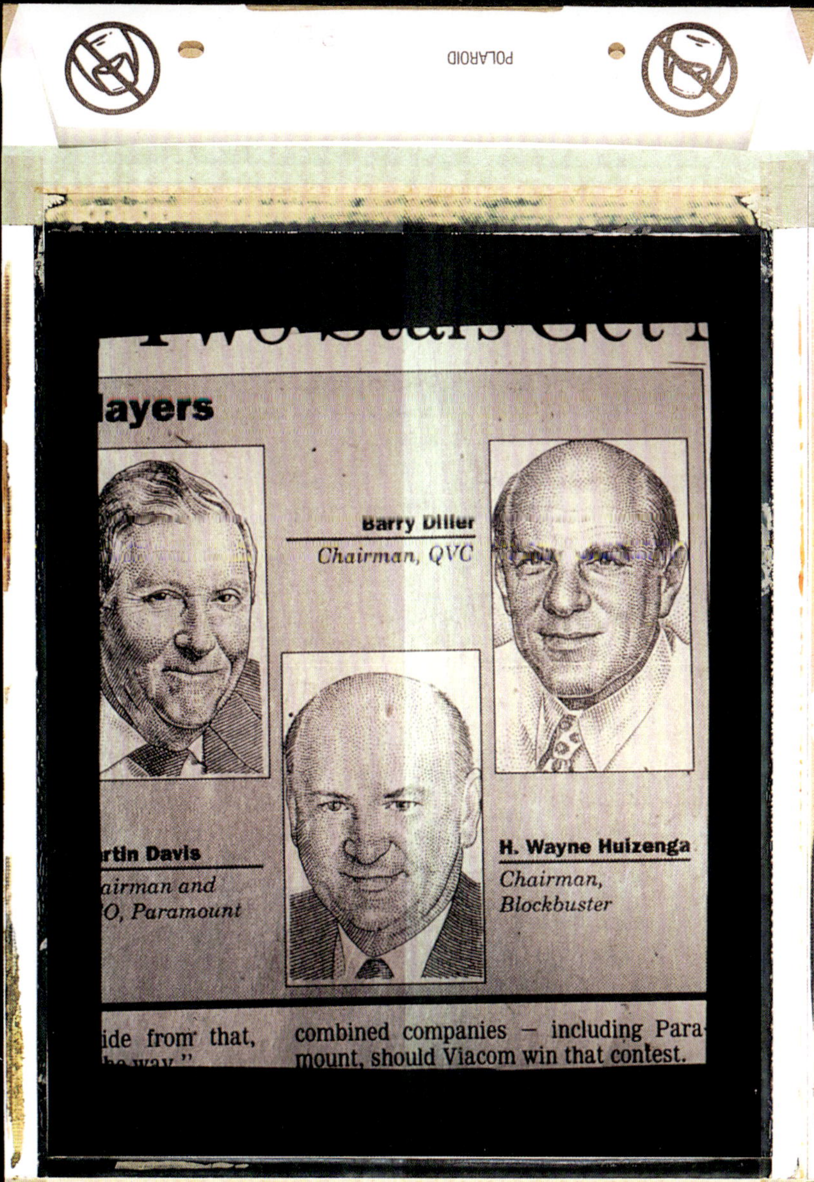

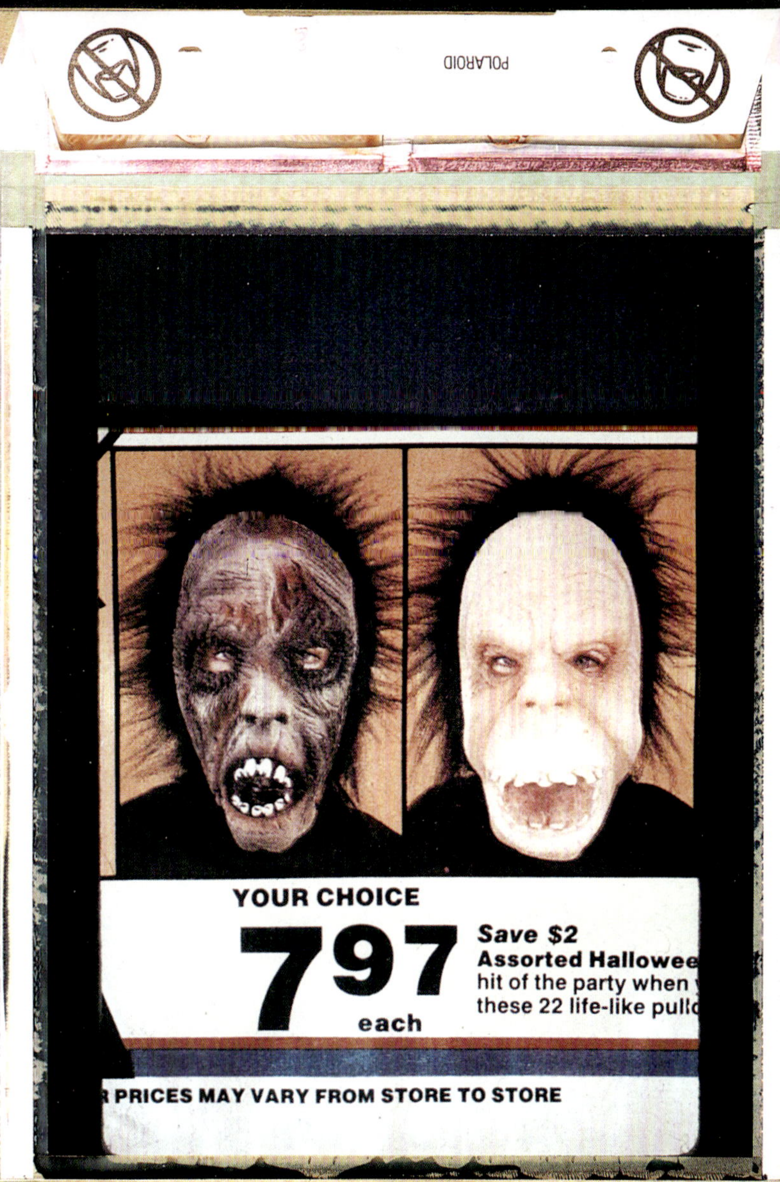

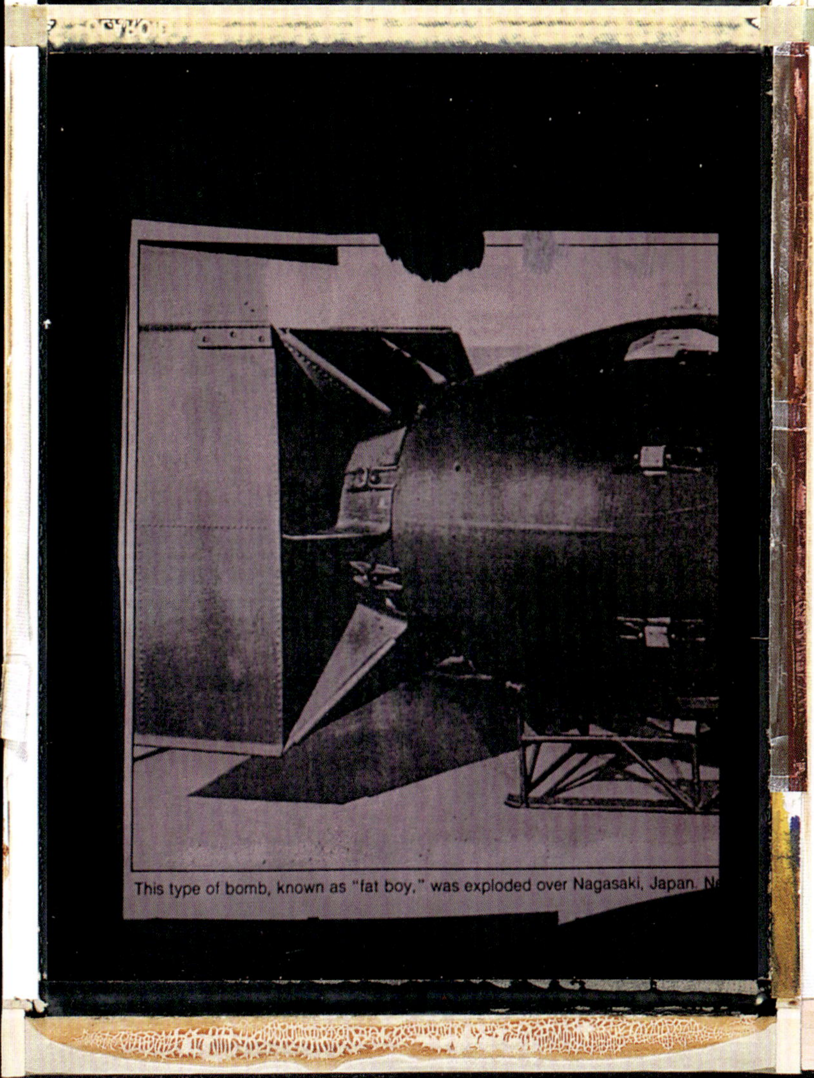

missing still: an animal of mind, higher, greater,
something to rule the rest: man is born:

the maker of things who made the better world
made him from diverse seed, or earth, fresh
from her own high air separation, kept
heavenly seed for this: mixed with rainwater by
Prometheus;
shaped into images of gods ruling everything

downward all animals look but man:
given sublime face to see sky, head
ordered erect to stars

once crude & imageless, earth changed, wore new
human shapes

A SEVENTH INNING STRETCH

BY RENNY PRITIKIN

As part of a series of gallery talks focusing on current exhibitions at the Ansel Adams Center for Photography, Center for the Arts Artistic Director Renny Pritikin was asked to address a work in Special Collections: The Photographic Order from Pop to Now, *a show organized by Charles Stainback of the International Center of Photography, New York. He responded with this meditation on the meanings of baseball, memory and art.*

UPON FIRST GLANCE, I assumed this anonymous collection was made of baseball cards. It was only when I saw the work at the Ansel Adams Center that I learned that it was made up of baseball phonograph records. Amazingly, I actually own a yellow plastic record of Jackie Robinson, Phil Rizzuto and others singing "The Umpire," which includes the classic lines, "The guy who calls every play, I ain't got no use for the umpire, unless he calls them our way." I thought I would write a little about baseball, and mention some things I have been reading and thinking about recently related to memory, taxonomy, museums, souvenirs and collections, and how this remarkable object of baseball memorabilia reflects these issues. If cultural theory at times imitates umpiring by the blind, I apologize in advance and admit that to call 'em the way I seen 'em is hopelessly compromised.

I remember seeing Mickey Mantle in the on-deck circle, the black number 7 stretched tightly across his back, the huge bull neck incomprehensibly strong to my preadolescent mind. I saw Roger Maris hit his 54th home run at Yankee Stadium the year he hit 61 to break Babe Ruth's record; my brother grabbed the scorecard and pencil out of my hand and wrote a big 54 on it. I was watching the 1960 World Series in my bedroom with Paul Knepper when Bill Mazeroski hit his home run to win the World Series for the Pirates. I was 11. Ken Boyer was a great third baseman for the Cardinals and so was his brother Clete, for the Yankees, but Clete couldn't hit. Clete was famous. Ken died young. Don Drysdale recently died young, too. Sandy Koufax was the best pitcher I ever saw. His curve ball would look like a wild pitch headed halfway between first base and home, then miraculously curl over the plate at 95 miles-per-hour. When I was a Mets fan it was a moral victory to get a hit off him before the fifth inning. I saw Warren Spahn pitch for the Mets when he was the age I am now. He won over two hundred games after the age of thirty. I attended Whitey Ford Day at Yankee Stadium and they had his relief pitcher, a Cuban guy, Luis something, climb out of a giant container of Lifesavers. I read an article in *Sport* magazine in the early '60s called "Don't Knock the Rock," about Rocky Colavito; I remember the bold sans serif type. He always stood in the batter's box pointing his bat directly at the pitcher until the pitcher went into his windup.

My wife and I were at a baseball game last year and the Giants right fielder, Willie McGee, came up to bat. My wife, feeling a little silly either from sitting in the sun for three hours or from massive boredom, leaned over to me and whispered in dead earnestness the non-sequitur, "Willie McGee, Bobbi McGee, Barry McGee." She was of course indulging in one of our favorite human activities: taxonomy, or according to the dictionary, the "science, laws or principles of classification." The group she was classifying was, of course, "all the people we know with the last name of McGee," with Bobbi being the subject of the Kris Kristofferson song and Barry being a wonderful young Bay Area artist. I was delighted by my wife's hilarious little list; I loved her for her quirky sense of humor, that shared moment epitomizing some of the fun of a long marriage. I loved it just because it highlighted the quixotic nature of human efforts to organize the world, in that this threesome probably could not have less in common other than the name McGee. Also, it was funny in the apparent completeness yet minuteness of its universe.

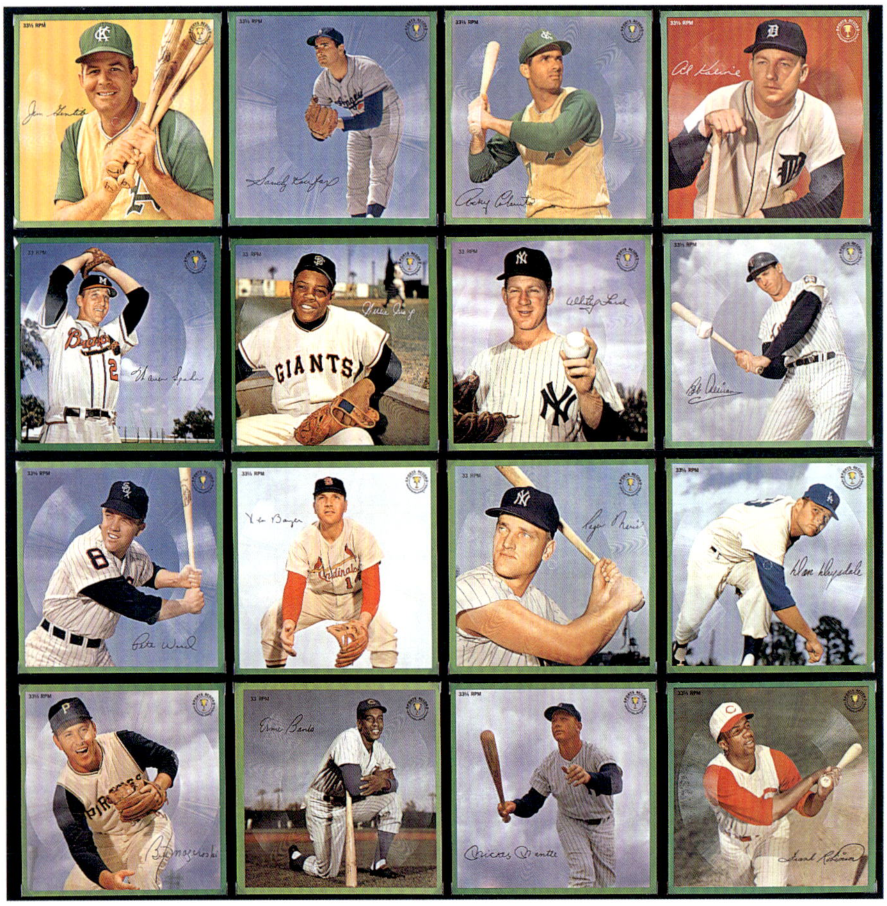

Photographer unknown, *16 Baseball Players,* 1962.

A month later, on vacation at Orcas Island near the Canadian border, I was writing. I hollered from the kitchen to my wife in the bedroom, asking her to recall her list of three names. She answered, "Willie McGee, Bobbi McGee and Fibber McGee." I intuitively knew that she had substituted Fibber for someone, but couldn't remember who. She insisted that her answer was the same as her original list, and we had a typical example of what can be classified as a "marriage argument." I hated her for an instant for stubbornly denying her (perfect!) Fibber substitution, but the tides of marital relations are a whole other taxonomy.

Now I am writing at my computer at work at the Center for the Arts, recalling all this McGee stuff, so it forms a neat little geographical triangle from Candlestick Park to Orcas Island to my office downtown in San Francisco. This triangle morphs into a rectangle if we consider a fourth corner representing the physical location of you, the reader. What we have here is a touchingly human, doomed attempt to bring order to the chaos of our lives. Distance both in geography and time indeed can create and alter memory. This is one way of saying what it is that artists do: through selection, isolation and juxtaposition, they make small areas of order out of the chaos of experience. Many contemporary artists may reject this analysis and embrace chaos, but these baseball portraits certainly indulge a nostalgia for order.

Dr. Robert Ornstein, who often writes on the human mind, holds that memory, dreaming and conscious thought all are different aspects of the same process. In his 1992 book *The Evolution of Consciousness,* Ornstein writes, "The world we experience, all the horses, the leaves, the coffee, the sunrises, the remembrance of things past, is all a dream of the mind... Our experiences, percepts, memories are not of the world directly but are our own creation, a dream of the world, one that evolved to produce just enough information for us to adapt to local circumstances." One of the profound implications of such an analysis is that memory is much less dependable than we think it is, that it is a blend of stored visual and emotional impulses on the same order as dreams, instincts and beliefs.

In her 1993 book *On Longing,* Susan Stewart distinguishes between the souvenir and the collection, in large part on the basis of their respective relation to memory. The souvenir is a scrapbook item, an object which takes us back to the past, often to a specific travel site, and which is incomplete in itself. It only takes on meaning when connected to a narrative, a retelling of the story of its origin. A collection, on the other hand, creates a self-contained world which looks to the future and creates a new context. The ultimate example of a collection is Noah's Ark. In 1989, Nayland Blake and I organized a show of eccentric collections at New Langton Arts, a San Francisco gallery. In his catalog essay, Blake suggested that we can distinguish two categories of collecting: that which has the goal of collecting the *most* and that which seeks to collect the *best.* That which collects the most is the natural history museum, wherein the ultimate goal is to collect everything, at least in miniature. The obsession to collect the best, rarest, most beautiful or most archetypal, fuels the impulse to collect one perfect thing. This is the model of the art museum.

Is this anonymous piece a collection or a souvenir? Stewart lays out two tests for a collection: it must argue for the part displacing the whole (the best players rather than all the players), and it must invent a taxonomy in space and time(United States, 1955-70, major leagues). So this piece can be seen as a small collection; one, however, that is counterpoised to an elite collection of impossibly rare and expensive items. Like a collection of salt shakers as opposed to fine jewelry, this collection speaks of middle-class values and original use value that was never inaccessible.

While partaking of the autobiographical elements of souvenir, this piece transcends mere autobiography and becomes social history. The narrative is not so much about places visited in the past by one person as it is about finding the common ground of shared social space and history.

I saw Al Kaline walk off the field right toward me, cradling his left arm in his right. I must've been sitting behind the visitors' dugout, at Yankee Stadium. He had tumbled over making a shoestring catch in right field, and broke his collar bone, out for the season.

Willie Mays was so much better than anyone else it wasn't fair. Like Duchamp, he didn't leave much for anyone else to do.

Stewart argues that as our experience becomes more and more mediated—that is, reflected, shaped, understood and even predicted by what we already have seen in mass media entertainment and advertising—our actual lived experience in our bodies, in relation to the world of phenomena we encounter, is replaced by a nostalgia for a purer, past time. The souvenir is evidence that there was such a time when our lives were real to us. There is no use value for souvenirs other than autobiography. This is particularly true of childhood souvenirs, for surely there is no greater nostalgia than that for childhood. We become tourists in our own pasts to escape the complexities of adulthood. Stewart concludes with the chilling passage, "The souvenir is destined to be forgotten; its tragedy lies in the death of memory, the tragedy of all autobiography... And thus we come again to the powerful metaphor of the unmarked grave."

Recently I heard a broadcaster tell the same story, only he got the details wrong—wrong field, wrong collar bone. It amazed me because I didn't think I shared that image with anyone else in the world. I saw Frank Robinson hit a ball into the gap for the Cincinnati Reds of '61, an incredible team. Vada Pinson, the other star hitter for the Reds, flew from first to home so fast it widened my understanding of what it could mean to be human. I remember seeing Pete Ward at third base in a powder blue road uniform the Sox tried for a while, and feeling embarrassed for him. Ernie Banks, one of the two or three best hitters of the '50s, played his whole career for the Cubs, who never even finished at .500. Jim Gentile pronounced it *genteel;* he must've been a favorite of the artist because he doesn't belong in this elite company. Willie Mays was so much better than anyone else it wasn't fair. Like Duchamp, he didn't leave much for anyone else to do.

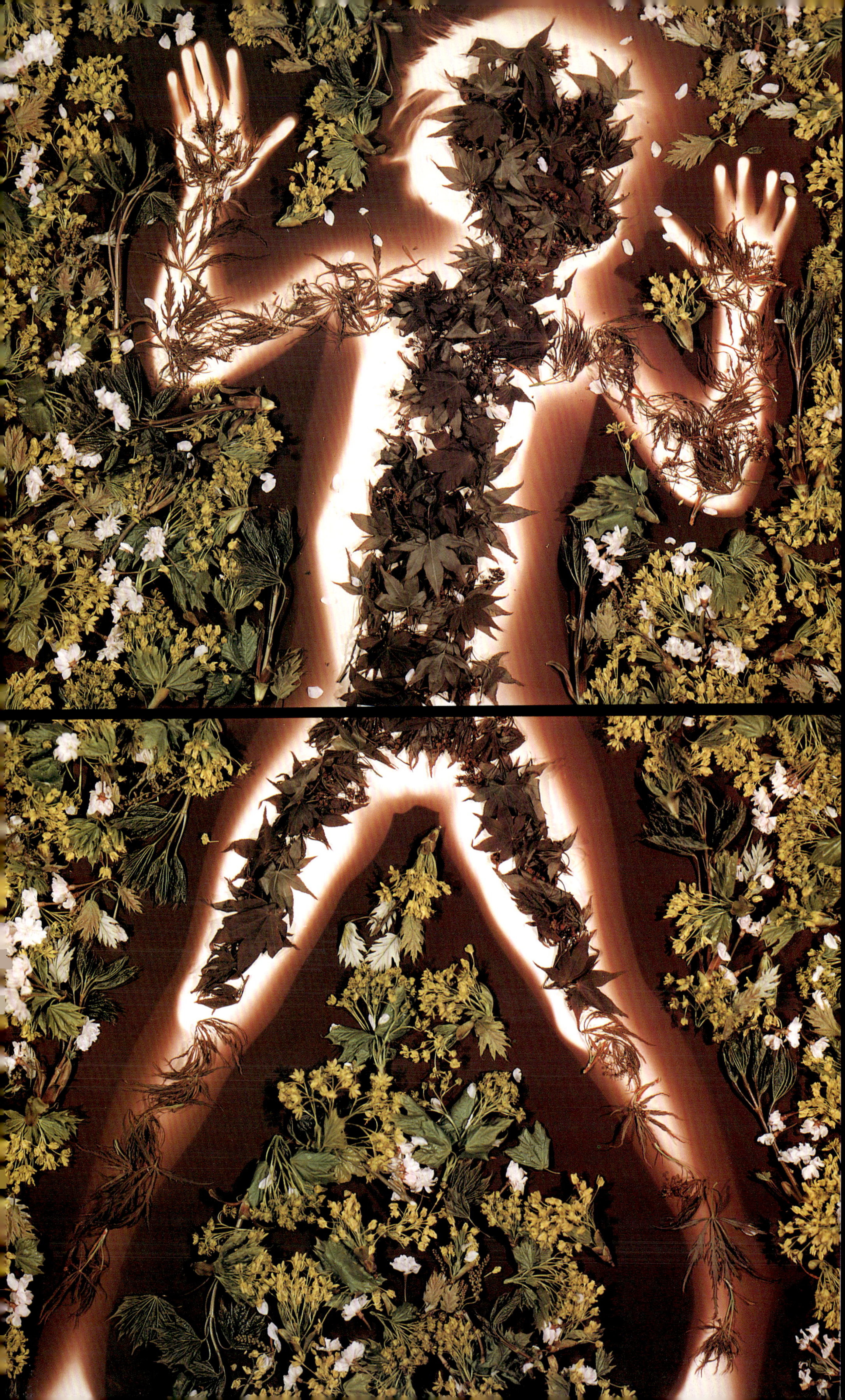

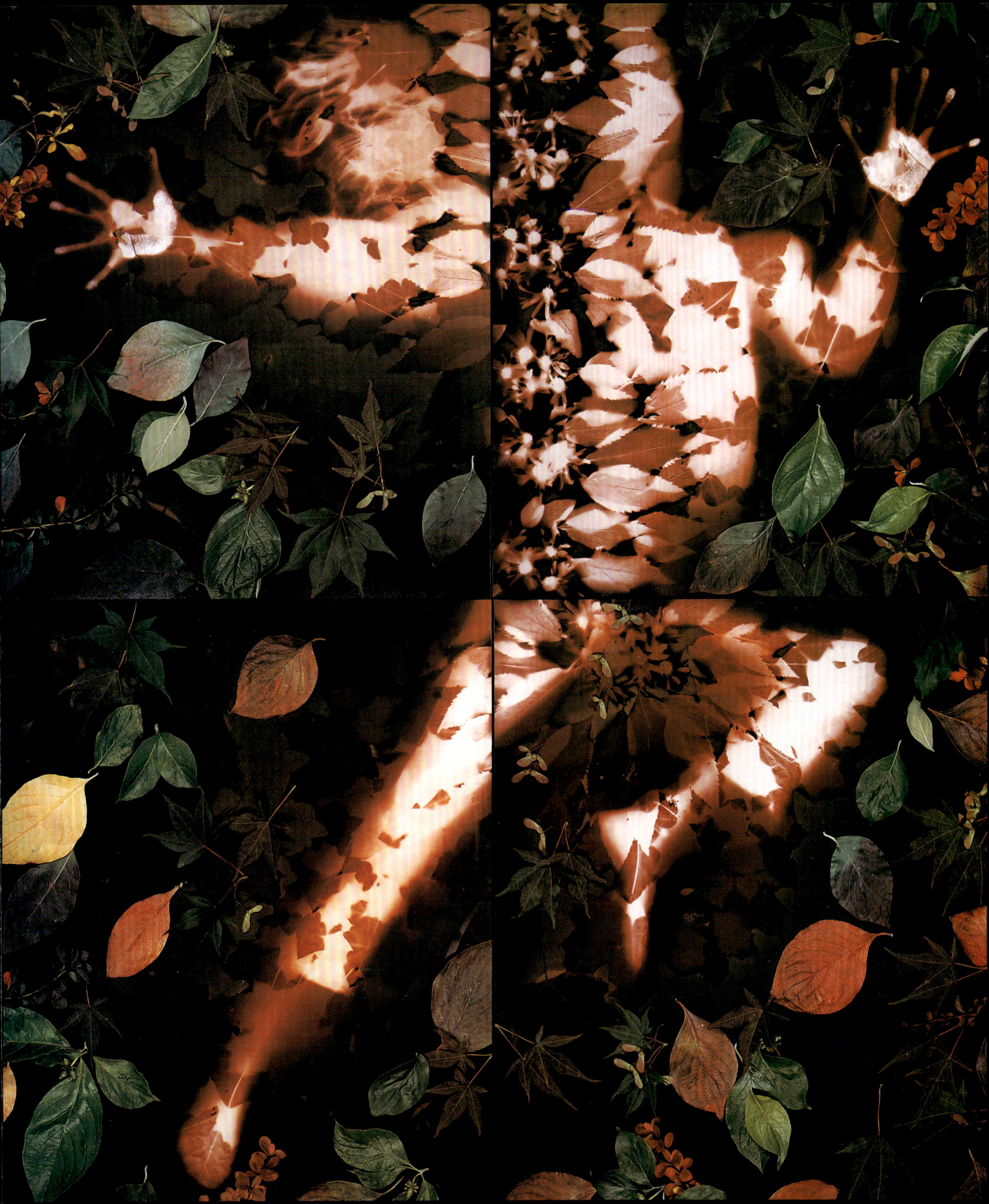

Clara, Autumn 1991/Summer 1994.

Facing page: *Spring (Grace)*, 1994.

MARTHA MADIGAN

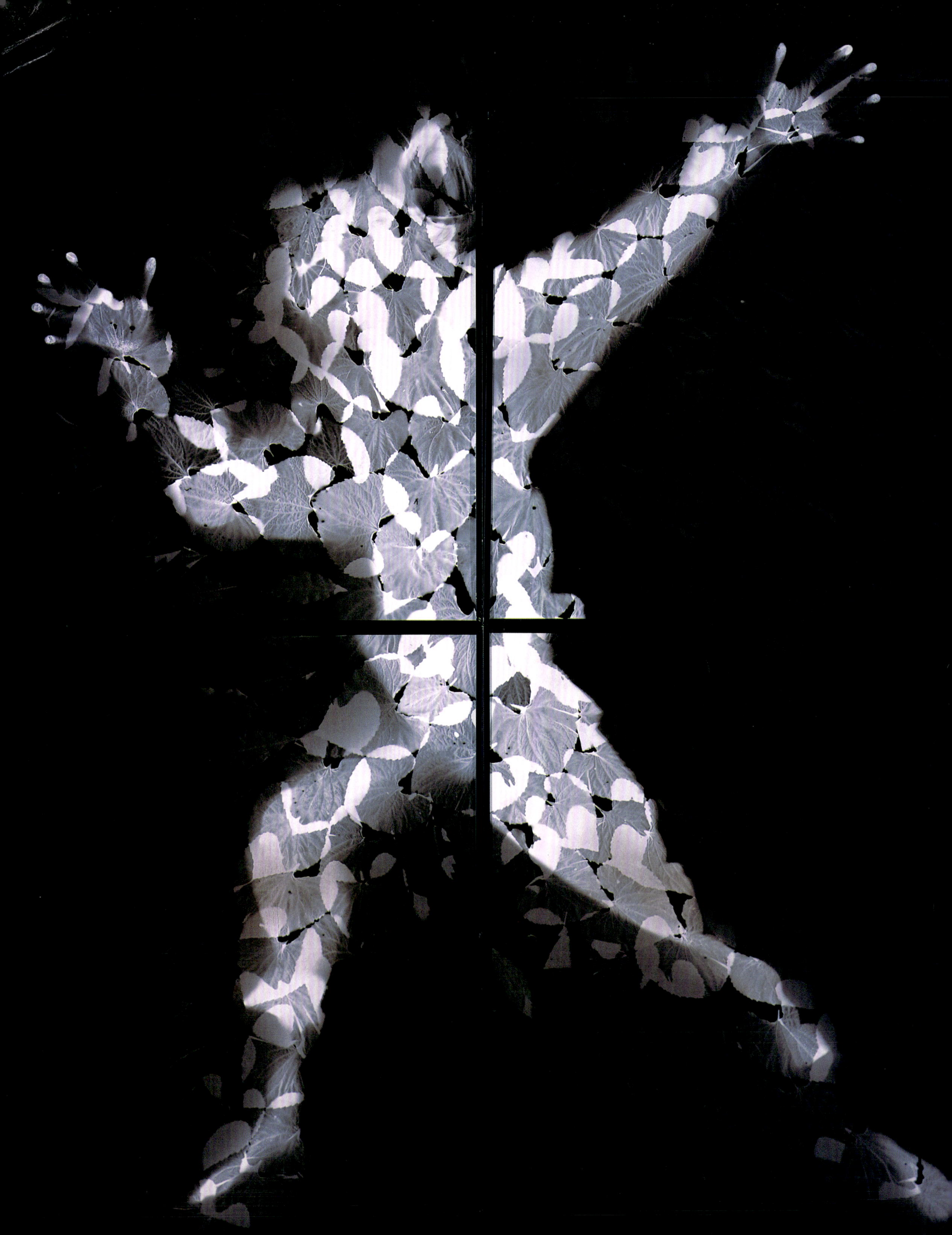

Daniel, Lost in Space, 1991.

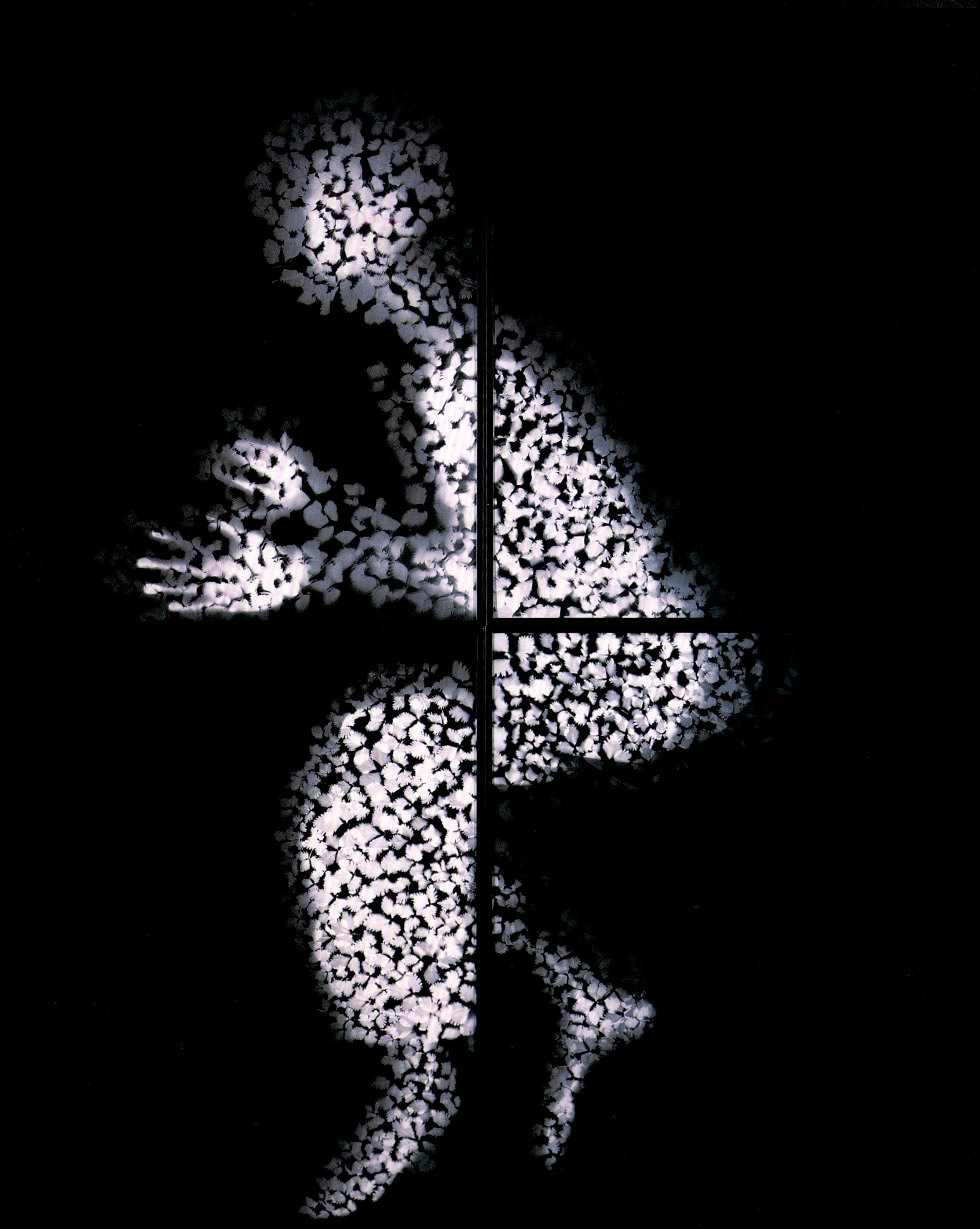

Grace, 1993.

WILLIAM JUDSON ZIPPER • ALEXANDER BELL TELEPHONE
• WILLIAM BURTON GASOLINE • CHARLES GINSBERG
VIDEOTAPE • WALLACE CAROTHERS NYLON • WILLIAM
CARRIER AIR CONDITIONING • WRIGHT BROTHERS
AIRPLANE • REGINALD FESSENDEN RADIO • RICHARD
GATLING MACHINE GUN • JOSEPH GLIDDEN BARBED
WIRE • CHARLES GOODYEAR VULCANIZED RUBBER •
GORDON GOULD LASER • JOSEPH HENRY ELECTRO-
MAGNET • **MICHAEL LIGHT** BLUE FALL • EDWIN LAND
POLAROID • WILLIAM SHACKLEY TRANSISTOR • CYRUS
McCORMICK MECHANICAL REAPER • GAIL BORDEN
CONDENSED MILK • JOHN DEERE STEEL PLOW •
J. ROBERT OPPENHEIMER ATOM BOMB • CHRISTOPHER
SHOLES TYPEWRITER • PERCY SPENCER MICROWAVE
OVEN • CHARLES BIRDSEYE FROZEN FOOD • ELISHA OTIS
ELEVATOR • ELMER SPERRY GYROSCOPE • LOUIS SULLI-
VAN SKYSCRAPER • PETER GOLDMARK COLOR TELEVI-
SION • PRESPER ECKERT ELECTRONIC COMPUTER
• NIKOLA TESLA ALTERNATING CURRENT • GEORGE
WESTINGHOUSE AIRBRAKE • ELI WHITNEY COTTON GIN

SUNDAY ROUNDUP
BY DAVID BRESKIN

An eco-sensitive minimalist, he tagged his targets
on oversized Post-it notes. Cops could never make
the graffiti charge—willful defacing—stick.

Unison riffing must be accompanied by a skullcap.
The new F-16s carry *Fire and Forget* missiles, so pilots
can concentrate on their subsequent tasty targets.

My dog's on drugs. This morning she said to me,
A wedding is just like a funeral without the dead
body. Sick as a dog, a dustmop with legs, Daisy.

A pissed blue-collar stiff with a tourniquet tie
says on the talk show, She don't deserve welfare.
Babysitters, Jobs, he pustulates. Ninety percent

of all welfare recips are unmarried women. Frisky
matinees show nuns scowling at redheads and blondes
in spangled minis doing the frug while the boys

in the Coke-bottle glasses pony awkwardly. Fear
always has a reason. Upside down on El Capitan,
out of rope, capilene undies not wicking correctly,

synchilla pilling and day-glo booties glaring in mean
Sierra sun, for instance. A low buzz like fuzz face
in your amp, intermittent. A pipe bomb in your lingerie

catalog, at large among the end-of-summer specials.
The portly ex-coach buttons his vest against angioplasty,
clears his epiglottis, and returns to the color. No one

can deny a lot of life is poorly shot. The grizzled vet
with ruptured spleen and eye damage audibles at the line
of scrimmage while water-fetching Bolivian girls ask

for your help in lush but stark Sunday slick rags.
A cross word for the Contras is discouraged. Meanwhile
back on Wall Street, the expansionist CEO of American

Airlines vows never to buy another plane. So burned
he's currently in treatment. Whole mountains of debt
and no pitons except in stomachs on line at unemploy.

For the role of her boyfriend his chest got waxed. Men
come at you with rotating knives and sucking hoses
in the middle of REM sleep. Why not clean your grandma

with Q-tips and toothbrushes like they would a car
in Bel Air? God is in the detailing. Pinstripes
bleed like Red Wings gung ho for fisticuffs. Violence

shows the absence of power, quote unquote. Tell that
to the lady whose leg was brightly snipered yesterday.
The body song continues: those with bifocals fall

on escalators, Teddy Roosevelt liked to tap-dance,
a one-pound spool of spider web would unroll all the way
around the world. Some men only enjoy sex with breast

cancer victims and now there is a magazine especially
for them. The ads are Miesian. Not a cell in your body
was there seven years ago. The suggestion of change

is plausible. Even snoring can be cured with a simple
procedure: uvulopalatopharyngoplasty. The old party,
licking their right-wing mandate, warns that peace

is seductive but will just lead to war. Until Arafat
shaves, they won't believe it. In seven years, a whole
new snorting herd of cells. Same old, same old. Saxes

on vinyl cue the dark chemicals, which drop the velvet
curtains on the thrust stage, draw a warm and soapy bath
for the mind, and snuff the mirrored candles like hit men.

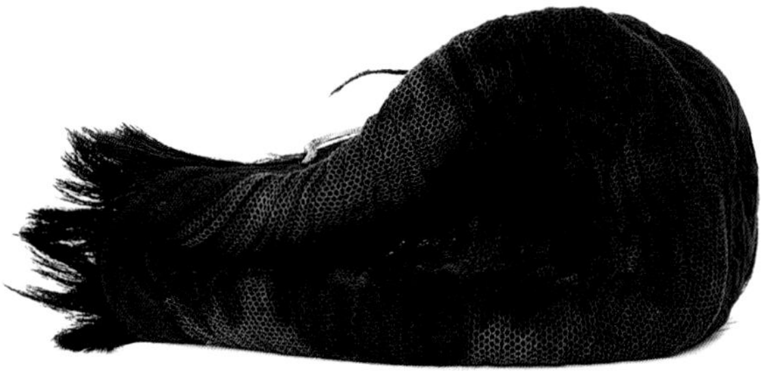

INSCRUTABLE OBJECTS

THE FIXITY OF THE PHYSICAL WORLD has been in question long before the words "virtual reality" were uttered. Our late twentieth century, post-industrial landscape is littered with the lingering detritus of Einstein's theory of relativity and, equally important, the third law of thermodynamics. Over time things fall apart, as the forces that bind them together decay and dissolve. Within this dissolution of molecular bonds and moral certainty can be found a fragile and tragic beauty appropriate to an age in which representation itself seems to be devolving. ● The images gathered together here are first of all symptoms of a loss of faith in the ability of objects to represent clear-cut meanings. Familiar territory is decontextualized and rendered alien, autonomous, threatening. Functionality is contested at every turn. The shoe no longer fits. Fruit and flesh switch places. Insides turn out. Holes open up in the seamlessly smooth skin of tangibility. These artists invite you not so much to look at the world differently, but to look at a different world. ● Traditionally, the still life genre has been a site in which the existing cultural values that are attached to familiar objects have been presented and confirmed. Usually, at least in Western culture, the explicit subject of the still life is materiality and mortality. Photographs in this genre testify to the concept of *Vanitas,* the principle that one's worldly possessions are inescapably subject to the contingencies of the flesh, and thus are of little consolation. In these still-life photographs, however, the material world is rendered so ambiguous and shifty that our preconceived notions about what things signify are unhinged. The iconic presentation of the objects adds to their mystery: they seem to aspire to an importance out of all proportion to their significance. ● What makes them suitable and worthy to be subjects for the camera is one question worth pondering. And there is another: Which are the real inscrutable objects, the things portrayed or the photographs themselves?
—Andy Grundberg

Jo Ann Callis, Untitled, 1992.

Facing page: Janice Tannin, Untitled, 1992.

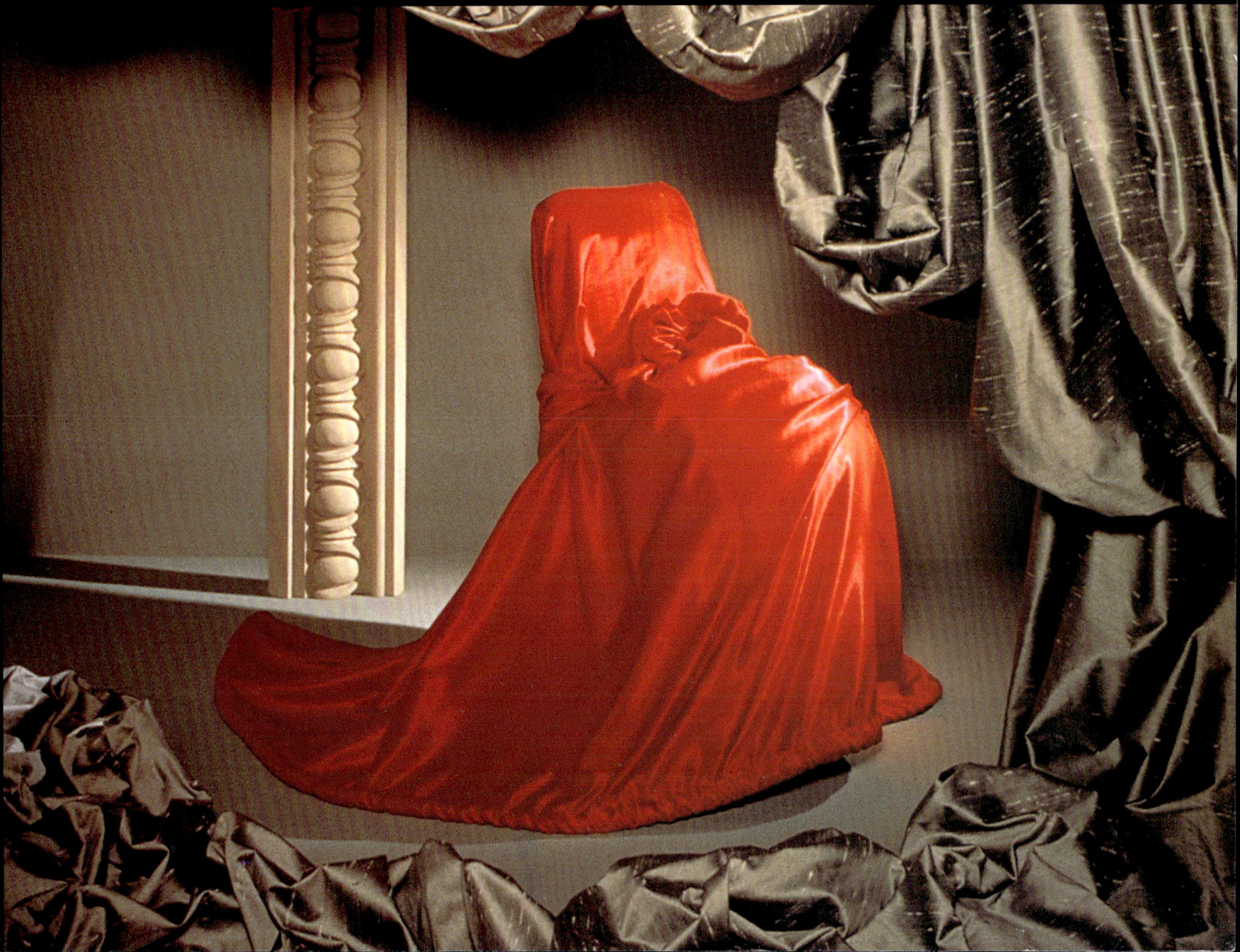

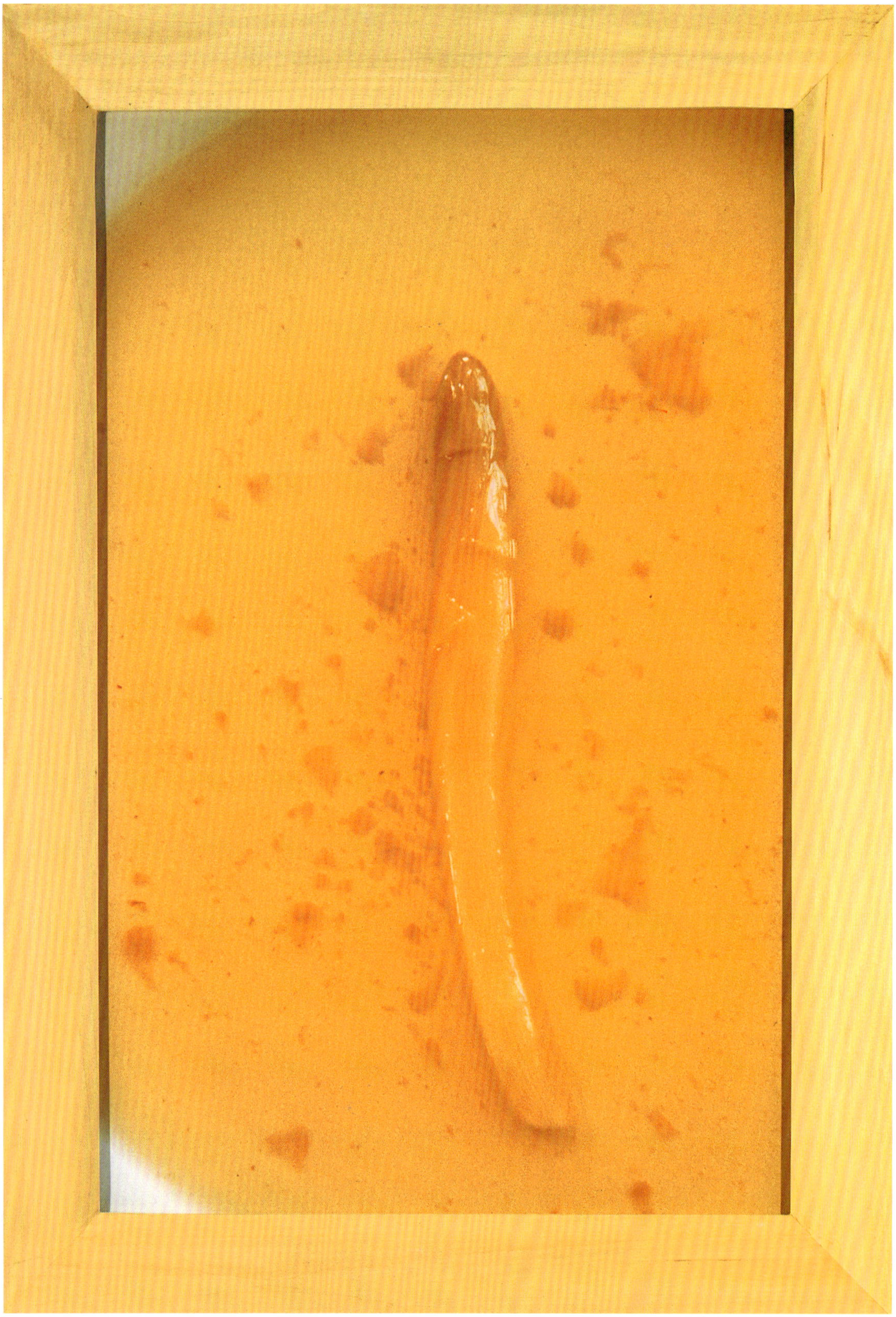

Jeanne Dunning, *Sample*, 1990.

Facing page: Ann Mandelbaum, Untitled, 1992.

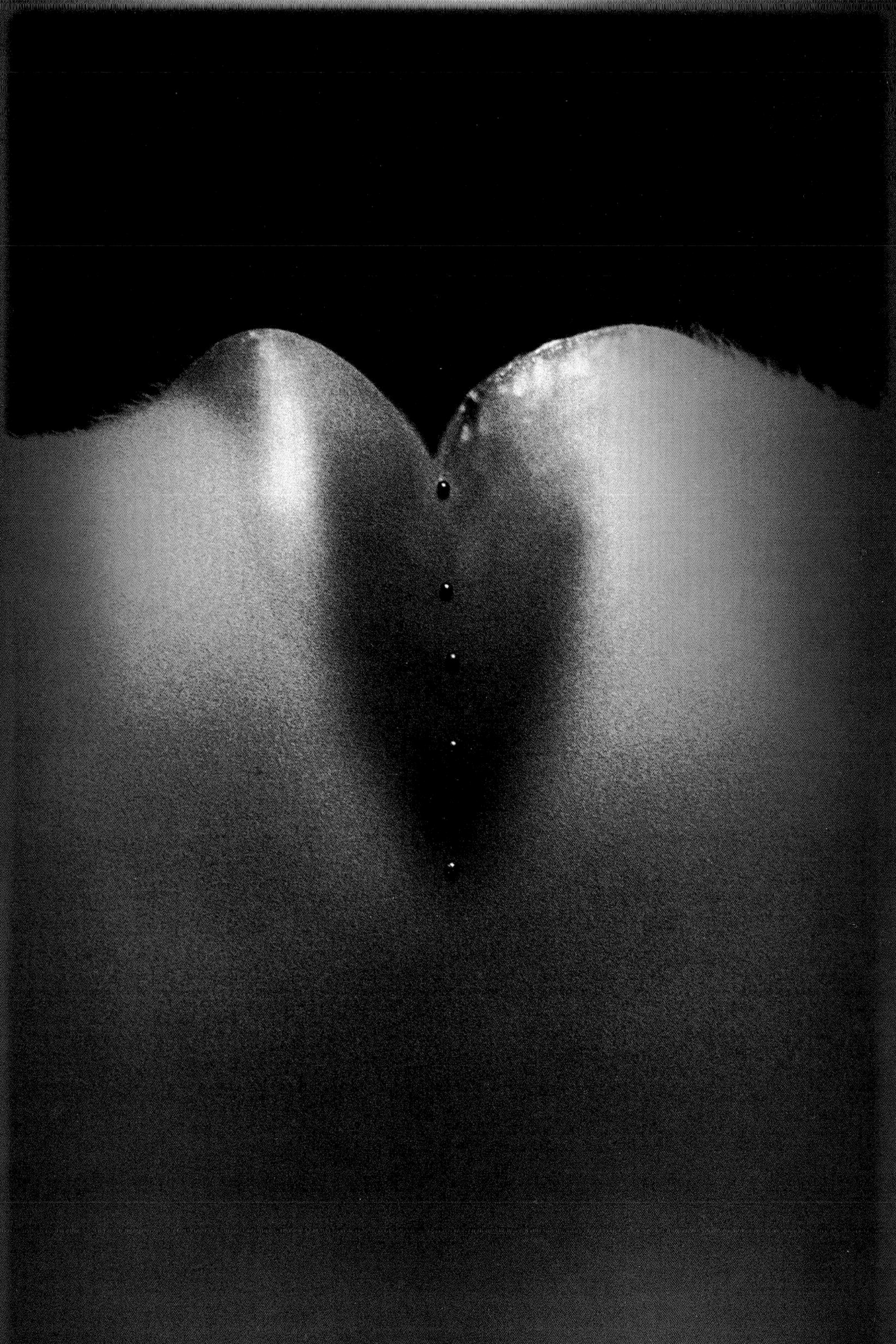

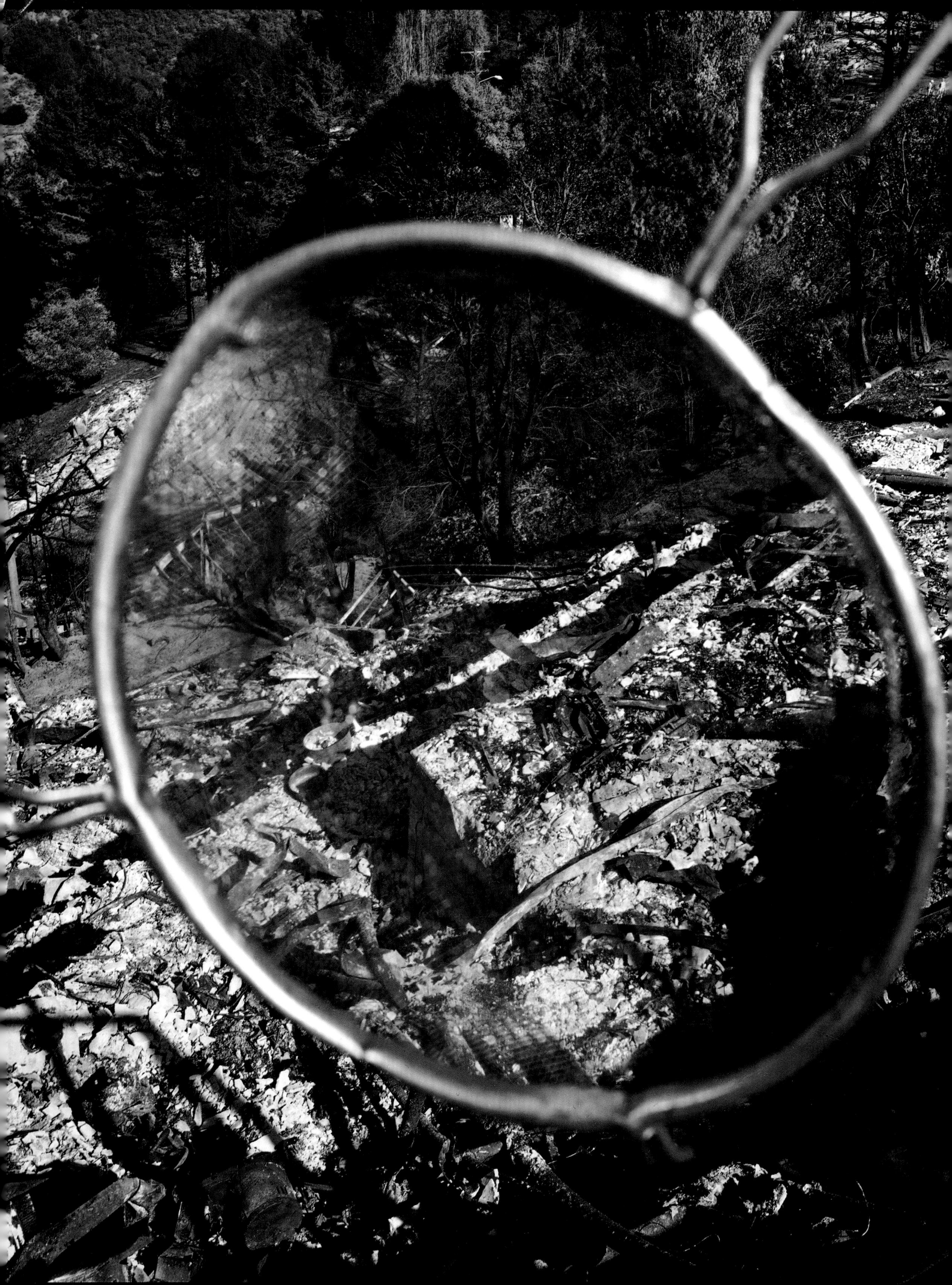

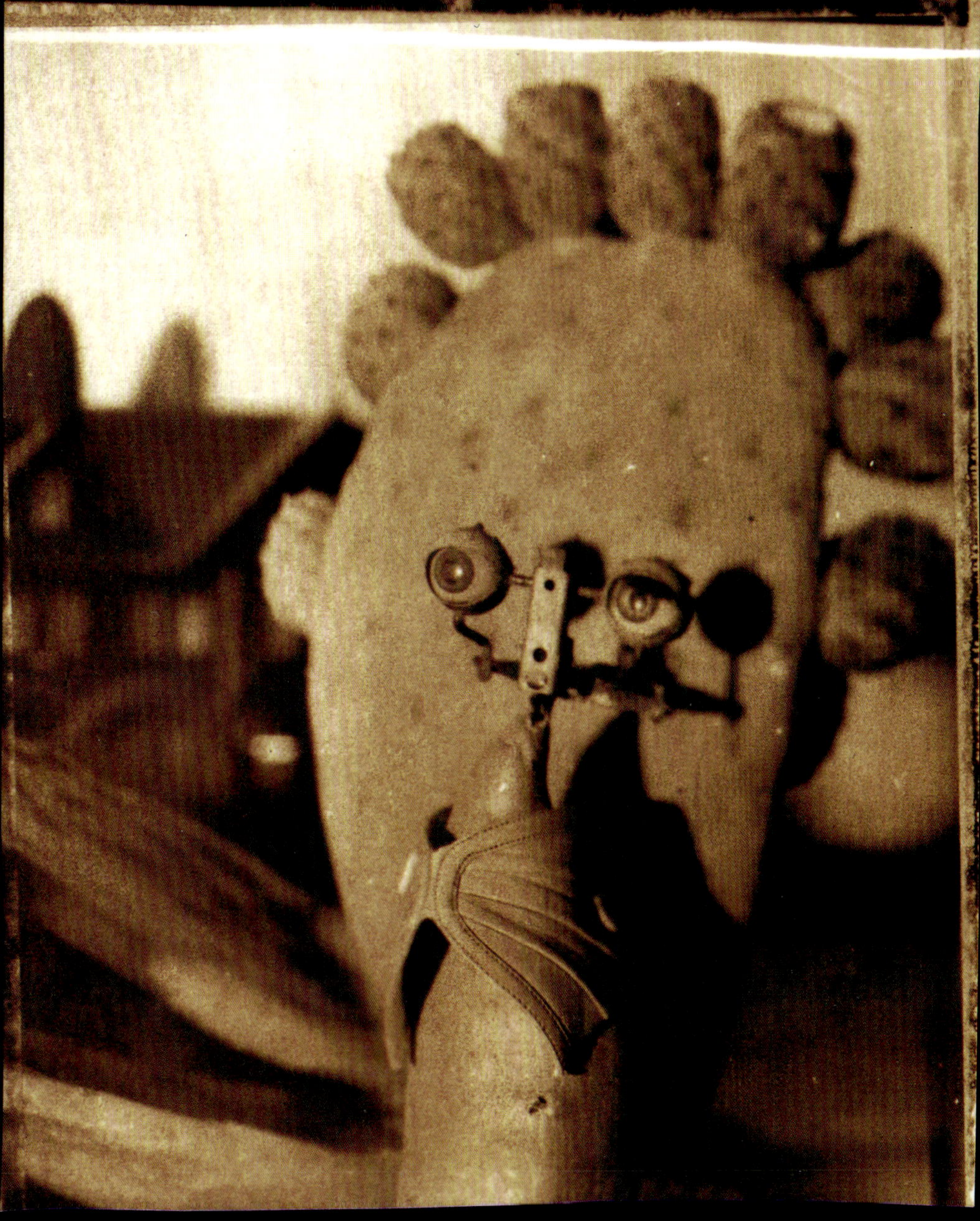

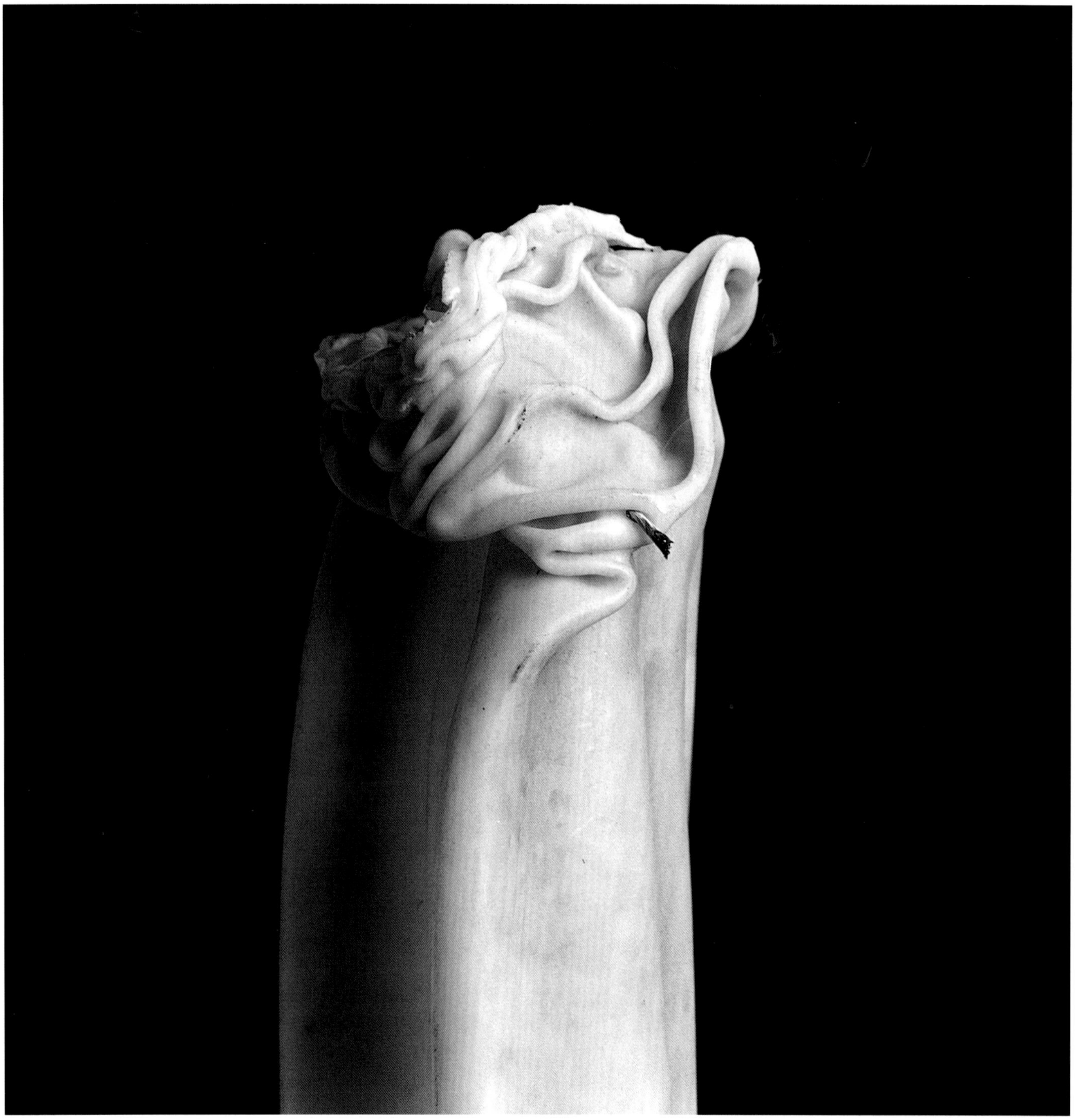

Elliot Schwartz, *Mapplethorpe*, 1989.

Facing page: Gay Outlaw, *Grande Poubelle*, 1994.

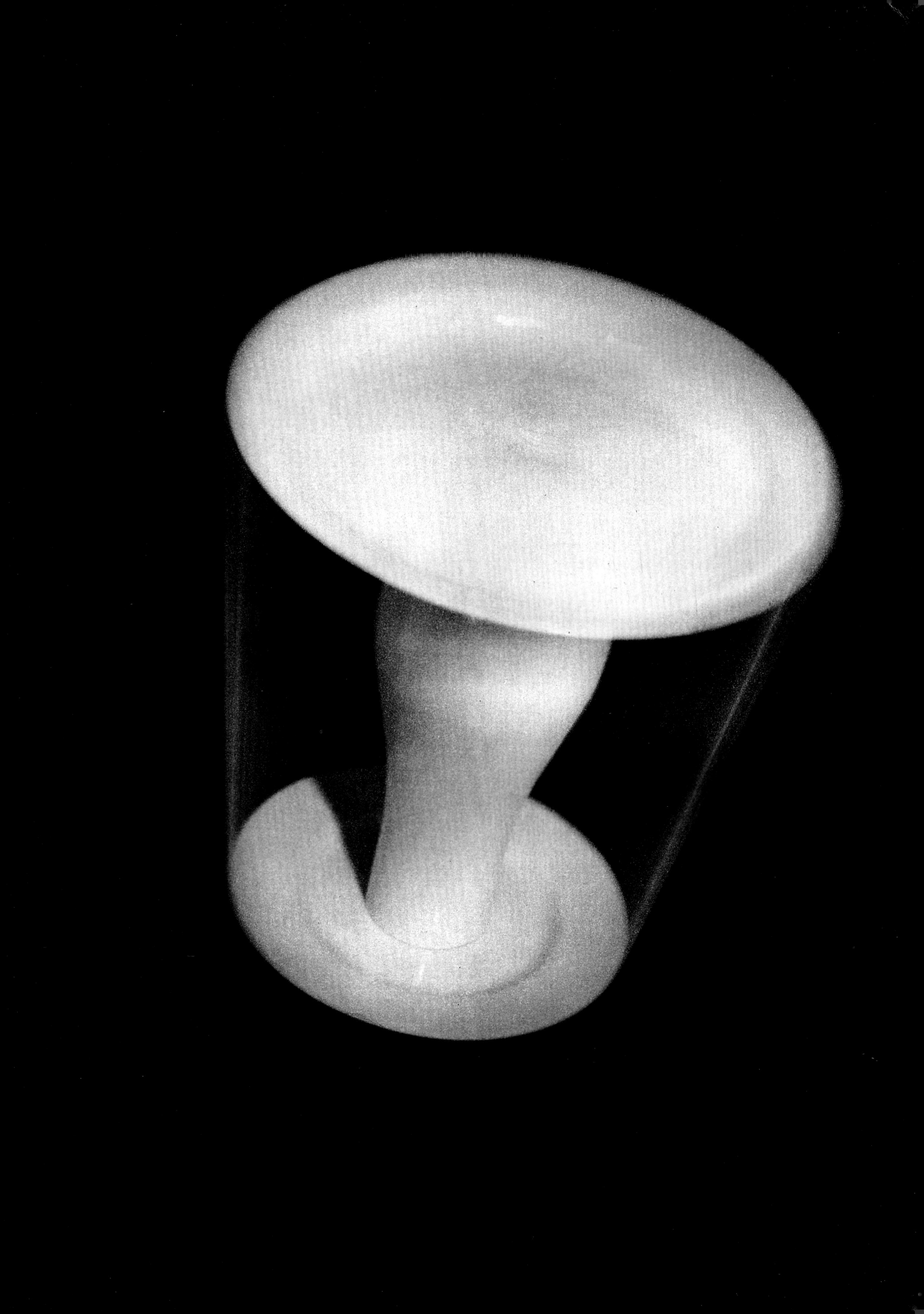

André Kertész

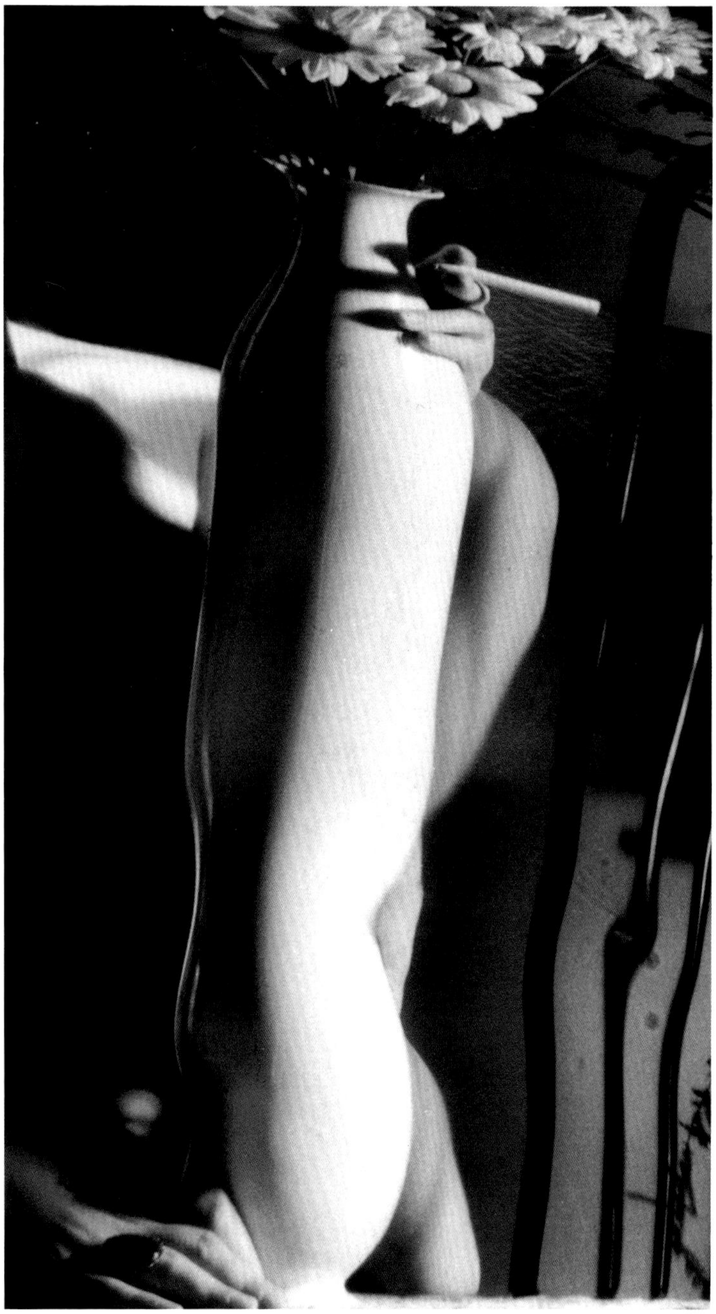

André Kertész, "Vase Distortion," Ca. 1936
13-3/4" x 7-1/4" Vintage Gelatin Silver Print Signed Mount Recto, Copyright Stamp Mount Recto

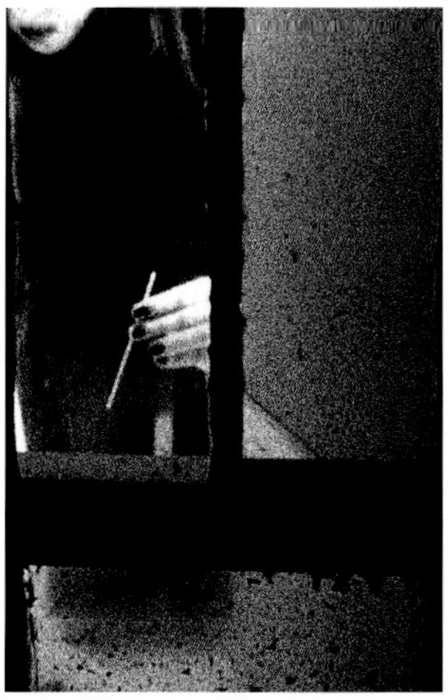

Merry Alpern, Window Series, 1994

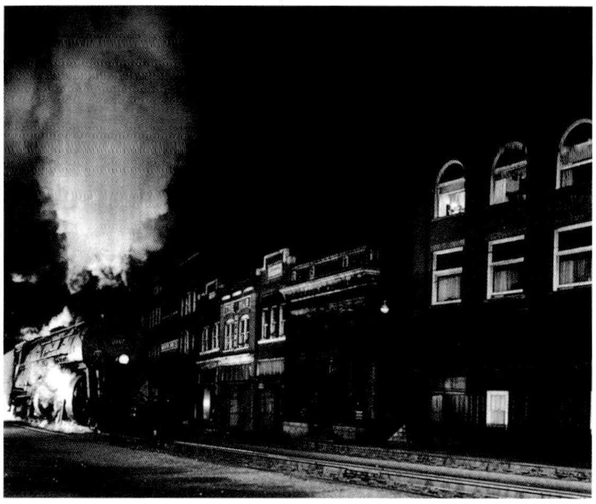

MAIN LINE ON MAIN STREET, NORTHFORK, WEST VIRGINIA, AUGUST 29, 1958

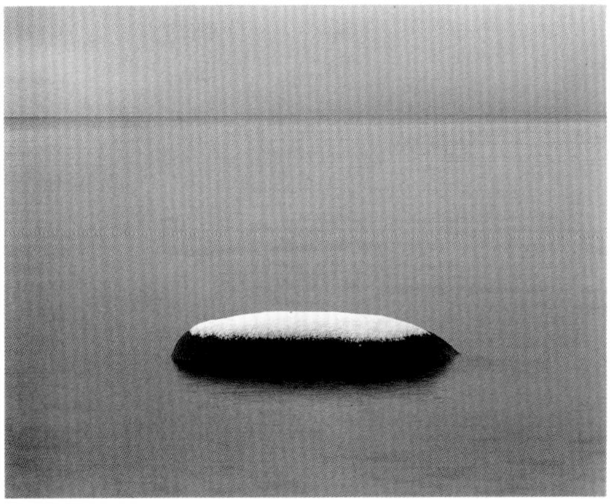

Snow Capped Rock, Lake Tahoe 1992

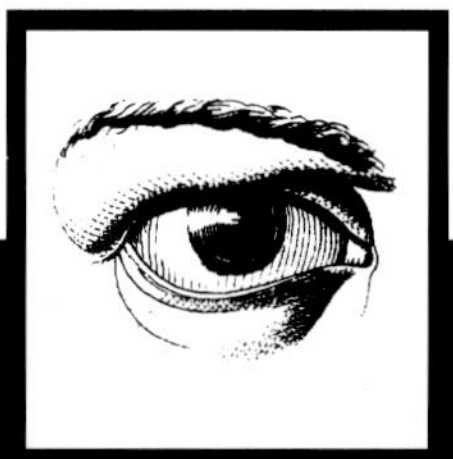

IN PRINT

Africa **by Herb Ritts**
Introduction by Judith Jamison
Bulfinch Press/Little, Brown & Co., 1995

Review by James Crump

It is important to realize, first and foremost, that they're human beings with hearts and souls and minds. They were so gracious to allow Mr. Ritts to become part of their existence, and they part of his—a shared experience that is AFRICA.

—Judith Jamison, from her Introduction to *Africa*

The mythological figure of "the Negro," who was always excluded from the good, the true, and the beautiful in Western aesthetics on account of his otherness, comes to embody the image of physical perfection and aesthetic idealization in which, in the canonical figure of the nude, Western culture constructed its own self-image.

—Kobena Mercer, from *How Do I Look? Queer Film and Video*

As we lunge towards the new millennium, the African continent, like much of the non-Western world, reels with changes brought forth by the internationalization of markets, the export of Western-style democracy, and high capitalism. Caught between its own bloody political and social instability and the pressures to become part of the "developed" world community, Africa continues to be viewed by Western observers with anxiety, apprehension and bewilderment. Paradoxically, Africa long has been perceived as the site of the mysterious, the "primitive," the mythological, as well as the exotic and erotic. Located at the nexus of sublimity and exploitation, Africa never has ceased to nourish Western desire and prurient fascination. It is this constant interplay between the dangerous and the magnetic attraction to the unknown (or unknowable) that informs our need to possess Africa—not simply through physical domination and economic control fostered by our colonial legacy, but also through our will to appropriate the continent's inhabitants and culture. How else can we explain the multitude of photographers who have supplied the Western psyche with views and impressions that form such a powerful collective fantasy of place? Naked black bodies at work, in the village, in the landscape and with their ritual objects and icons, were the stock-in-trade of photographers who were dispatched to Africa during the height of European colonization.

Today, however, these African specimens of ideal beauty and grace need not be gathered as documents under the aegis of anthropology or ethnography. In the late-twentieth century, it is through the gaze of commercial and fashion photography that the West prefers to consume Africa.

Following in the footsteps of photographers such as Leni Riefenstahl and Irving Penn, Herb Ritts is the most recent figure to feast upon the visual inventory that has become the stereotype of the "Dark Continent." Known primarily for his fashion, advertising, portrait and video work, Ritts was sent on assignment by Levi's to Morocco and subsequently was lured on an African safari. He was suitably impressed: "Taken with certain elements of the place: the light, the texture, and the expanse of land," Ritts fell in love with the people, "their dark skin, their glow, and their warmth." [1] The place is East Africa, primarily Tanzania and Kenya. And the people are the Maasai, the nomadic herder society recognized for the fecundity of its male warriors and its strong resistance to cultural change. Two journeys to the region and seven thousand negatives later, Ritts' elegantly printed photo book and exhibition, *Africa,* suggest that the Modernist paradigm of "salvage ethnography" is not only alive and well, but perpetually marketable to disinterested Westerners with spendable incomes.[2] To be intoxicated by this richly designed book is to ignore where the photographs ultimately originate and their sordid connection to the colonial past. Like his innumerable predecessors, Ritts clings to the worn-out notion of Africa in a pre-civilized state, reducing the beautiful black face and body to fetish objects that are offered up to Western viewers for aesthetic appraisal.

Like Penn's 1984 volume, *Worlds in a Small Room,* Africa now casts ambulant celebrity photographer Ritts as the "artist" busy at work in foreign environs. Separated in time by a decade, both books demonstrate the power of creative artifice and the perennial importance and appeal of the pose. What emerges is the politics of style earmarked to glamorize a professional reputation; the book is meant to be perceived as a serious enterprise that transforms Ritts into an "art"photographer, and hence a "collectible" photographer.

Transfigured by his camera, the dramatic faces and bodies that Ritts chooses to portray possess an unsettling relationship to his work for *Vogue* and *Vanity Fair.* Working in the shadow of Rousseau, Gaugin, Picasso and a host of Modernists before him, Ritts simply refines the primitivist model. He blends his aesthetic response with the force of "realism" and quasi-documentary, as if he had discovered the Maasai in such glorious profiles and close-ups. Ritts seems to have forgotten that his repertoire has been exhausted on the likes of numerous film stars, athletes and models. The book is fettered by a psychological overlay of familiar images, recognizable as if in a dream. As more than one observer has noted, didn't Ritts pose Magic Johnson the very same way he portrays Correya, one of his recent African subjects? This portrait belies the intensity of Correya's existence, failing to suggest anything but Ritts' contrived projection of glamour. The calloused skin of Correya's hands and

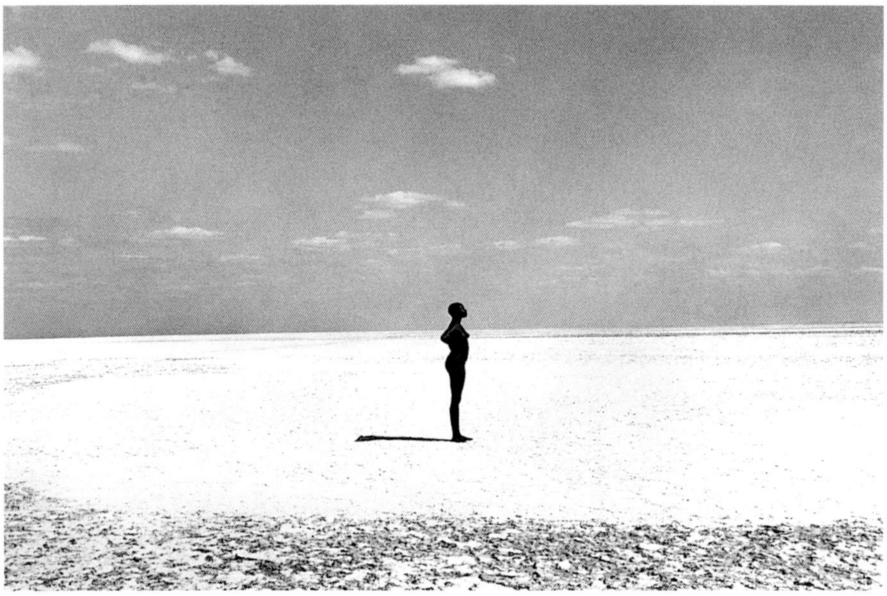

Herb Ritts, *Malaika, Profile, Manyara Salt Lake, Africa,* 1993. From *Africa.* ©Herb Ritts. Courtesy Fahey/Klein Gallery, Los Angeles.

wrists and his parched lips now are emblems of beauty and a good sense of design.

Similarly, Ritts presents the deformed foot of an elderly Maasai woman opposite the foot of a young warrior. Symbolic of social order and distinction, these feet suggest the weathering of time as well as wisdom, maturity and mortality. Ritts, however, can muster only editorial pastiche with these photographs, a formulaic recycling of his 1987 image of Olympic athlete and track star Jackie Joyner Kersee. When she's not seen holding a giraffe vertebrae, or bending her sensuous body in the Manyara Salt Lake, Ritts inserts his favorite female model, Malaika, into the time-tested pose typically reserved for the black male, as in the work of F. Holland Day and Robert Mapplethorpe. If we didn't know where she was from, Malaika easily could stand for any number of Ritts' celebrity nudes in which the body is artfully posed with objects such as pine branches, tumbleweed, shells and even an octopus.

Progressing from the faces and bodies of the Maasai to the textural design of nature and the exotic native wildlife, *Africa* is one successive jump cut after another—a carefully sequenced rhythm of immaculately printed photographs that strive for the frenetic pace of a fashion layout. The effect is typical of Ritts' publications and also calls to mind his earlier work in other media, chiefly his Janet Jackson music video that labored to reference non-Western tribal culture. The only real difference is the set location and the choice of models. Instead of viewing black bodies ritually frolicking to Jackson's thump and grind in the California salt flats, we now see the Maasai in their African desert; they are Ritts' latest stand-ins for his fantasy scenarios of chic cultural otherness.

As a disappointing result of so much time, money and resources, *Africa* is yet another project which only confirms white, ethnocentric consciousness, now updated and stylized for popular consumption. Safely distanced both by geography and the photographer's selective point of view, the reality of this part of the world— a culture facing irreversible change and fragmentation—is no more accessible to Western viewers than it was when colonization began. Any attempt to portray or interpret the politics, sociology or day-to-day lives of these people would have sullied the majestically hip presentation that Ritts obviously seeks. For all its vastness and diversity, Africa, at least according to Ritts' vision, remains the stereotyped bank of images resonating in our collective memories. *Africa* is a beautifully designed and sumptuously printed book, but nonetheless a fiction that only distorts meaningful efforts to understand Africans and their culture.

NOTES

1 Guy Cross, "Interview with Herb Ritts," *THE Magazine*, (November 1994), pp. 20-21.

2 The term "salvage ethnography" is borrowed from James Clifford's seminal work, *The Predicament of Culture: Twentieth-Century Ethnography, Literature, and Art,* (Cambridge, MA, Harvard University Press, 1988). See also *Writing Culture: The Poetics and Politics of Ethnography,* eds. James Clifford and G. Marcus (Berkeley, The University of California Press, 1986).

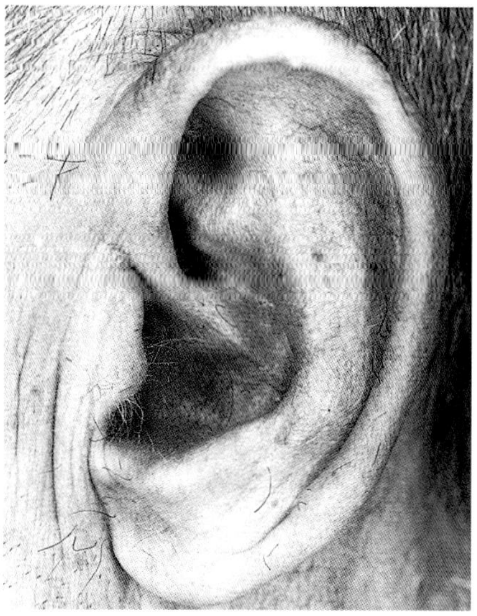

Robert Davies, *Ear 1,* 1992. From *The Body.*

The Body: Photographs of the Human Form
William Ewing, ed.
Chronicle Books, 1994

Review by Valerie Soe

Weighing in at three pounds and spanning 430 pages and a two-inch width, *The Body: Photographs of the Human Form* is packaged like a small bomb—dense, compact and full of hidden implication. Despite its considerable girth and handsome appearance, *The Body* is a surprisingly lightweight exploration of human physicality, affording few revelations about its subject. As a sampling of photographic representations of the human form, *The Body* is undernourished.

Like most Modernist art forms, photography's history almost always has been presented as a strict linear progression—one event logically leads to the next, early schools of work influence later ones, and artists dutifully build on the work of their predecessors. Taxonomically arranged photographic studies seldom stray from this chronological interpretation, grouping their subjects into historical progressions from point A to point B. *The Body* attempts to break down these familiar systems of organization. By grouping everything from Victorian daguerreotypes to medical scanner images to throwaway publicity photos in one mass of visual information, the book suggests a more innovative approach to photographic history. However, this apparently radical organizational strategy belies the fairly conventional contents of editor William Ewing's accompanying text.

By organizing chapters along thematic lines under headings such as "Fragments," "Probes," "Prowess" and "Eros," Ewing promises an unconventional view of photography of the flesh. Unfortunately, he abandons this potentially rewarding exploration of genres in favor of a more linear and familiar recounting of photography's development, from its scientific and anthropological beginnings through contemporary artistic practice.

Ewing's approach is typified in the chapter titled "Figures," in which he moves from nineteenth-century daguerreotypes and albumen prints to photographs by Alfred Stieglitz, Edward Weston and Imogen Cunningham, ending with images by Sally Mann and Robert Mapplethorpe. Likewise, "Idols" begins with turn-of-the-century bathing beauties, continues through Muscle Beach and concludes with Raquel Welch, cleverly juxtaposing historic plates with Hollywood publicity prints and Bruce of Los Angeles' photographs of beefy bodybuilders. Here, Ewing displays a knack for unlikely connections and a willingness to consider both art photography and paparazzi snapshots in his ruminations.

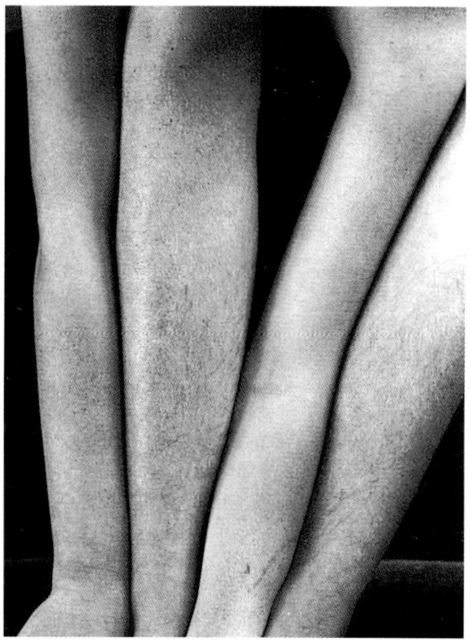

Edward Weston, *Nude, Charis, Arms and Legs,* 1934. From *The Body.*

The most arresting images in the book are neither by artists nor professional photographers, but rather are attributed to doctors and scientists who have used photographs of the human form for research. Scanner-produced images of the workings of the eye or the plates of the leg bone are startling and unexpected in their complexity. Ewing's inclusion of these images alongside those of Man Ray and other artists attest to photography's many applications beyond vanity, creativity and record-keeping.

The book's outstanding design elements—high-quality color and black-and-white reproductions, careful cropping and placement, fluidity of layout—are almost enough to distract the viewer from the shortcomings of Ewing's text, which often is merely descriptive and formalist. He is most successful when he leavens his analysis with historical background, as in his discussion of Dutch photographer Jo Brunenberg, whose photographs he compares to the scientific drawings of Leonardo da Vinci.

What damages *The Body* is its almost exclusive focus on images by Western photographers of Western bodies. Ewing's inclusion of photographs of other ethnicities is limited to a handful of anthropological photographs, two male nudes, a pair of Lorna Simpson pieces and an odd image of a Japanese letter-bearer in a dhoti. Ewing does manage to discuss the representation of non-Europeans by Western photographers, revealing for example that anthropologist F.R. Barton's pedophiliac proclivities overwhelmed his scientific detachment in his photographs of tattooed Papauan girls. Ewing also mentions photography's early, troubling use as a means of determining ethnic hierarchy, recalling how Europeans utilized photography's tendency towards subjectivity as proof of their own superiority.

Elsewhere, in his discussion of the loaded topic of eroticism in photography, Ewing sounds pedantic and dated as he takes great pains to differentiate between the prurient and the expressive. His earnest, polemical treatment of art and pornography reveals a stuffy conservatism: "A poetic eroticism, entirely void of licentiousness, suffuses the work of Ralph Gibson. . . . For Gibson, a woman's erotic power stems also from the way her body is groomed, dressed and adorned. His fragmentary perspective is not just a formal device—a means of indulging his love of abstraction—it is also a way of withholding, or holding back, and thereby deepening the sense of mystery. If any single factor separates the true eroticist from the pornographer, it is this." This hazy distinction between poetry and lust is incongruous, given the conscious blurring of boundaries between the two realms in the work of many photographers featured in *The Body.*

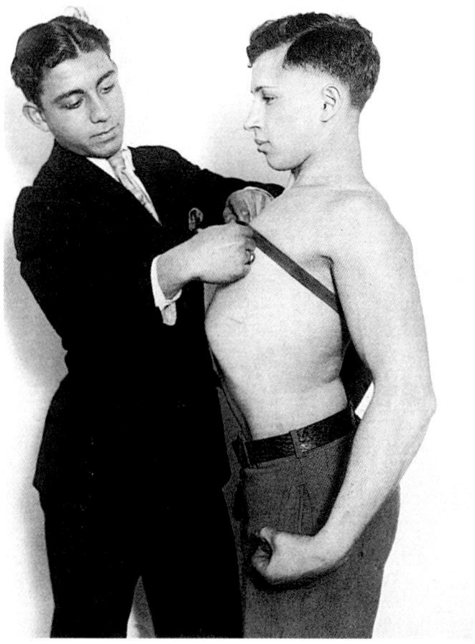

Anonymous, *The Strongest Boy in New York: Harry Luft,* 1926. From *The Body.*

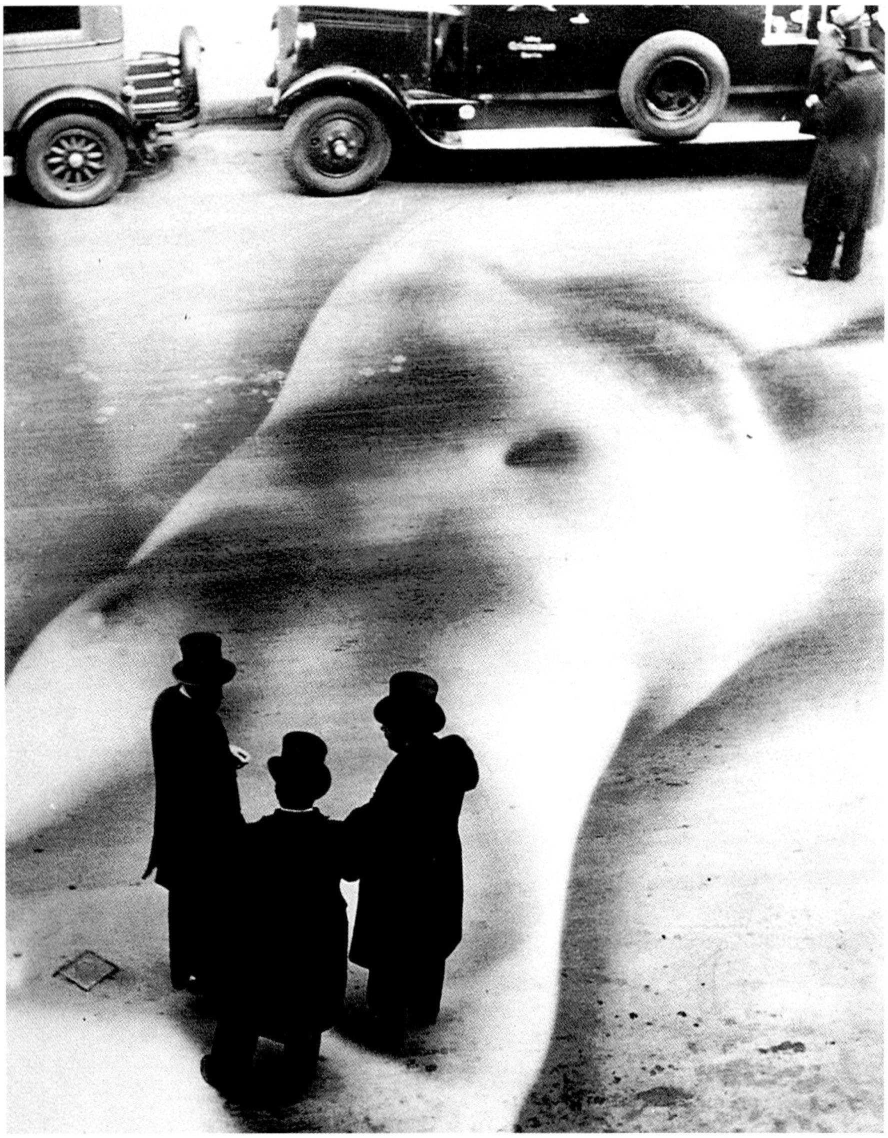

Heinz Hajek-Halke, *Double-exposure Nude and Street Scene,* c. 1927. From *The Body.*

Moreover, Ewing's refusal to acknowledge the value of titillation is unconvincing in this book filled with beautiful, sensual depictions of the human form. His protestations deny an integral reason for marketing such a publication in the first place: images of the human figure are pleasurable to look at. Splitting hairs between the high-minded intentions of *The Body* and pornography's supposedly baser motivations is disingenuous and pretentious at best, and Ewing's dismissal of photography's potential to stimulate both the higher and lower instincts discounts an important aspect of the work that *The Body* presumes to discuss. Ewing might do well to look more closely at his own statement, "Photographs of the figure are not always what they seem." Similarly, in the case of *The Body,* seemingly inventive approaches to the history of photography are not always as visionary as they seem.

American Politicians: Photographs from 1845 to 1993
Susan Kismaric, ed.
Abrams/Museum of Modern Art, 1994

Review by Dan Meinwald

Given the increasing ascendancy of media-manufactured image over substance in American politics, a book that profitably examines the role played by the photographic image in politics is long overdue. That book might ask, for instance—without arriving at a definitive answer—whether photography only mirrors transformations in the practice of politics, or has been a catalyst for change. It certainly ought to ask of the pictures it contains: Who made these photographs? Who first looked at them? In what context were they seen, and how did that context influence their interpretation? Unfortunately, *American Politicians,* a catalogue accompanying an eponymous traveling exhibition organized by Susan Kismaric at the Museum of Modern Art, is not that book. Kismaric's attempt to examine the photographic representation of American politicians does little more than skim the surface of a complex subject.

This shortcoming appears to be a result of the kinds of questions Kismaric asks, and does not ask, of the photographs she chooses, and the kinds of answers she comes up with. Why, for example, is this book about politicians, and not politics? Part of the answer is simple: it is far easier for a photographer to depict a person than an abstraction. Nevertheless, is the concentration on personalities, both in politics and in this book, entirely a product of the requirements of representation, or might there be other causes? In fact there are. They have to do, on the one hand, with definitions of the individual, and of the place of the individual within society and in the development of America's national identity. They also have to do with a theory of history that grants significance only to the thoughts and actions of those who wield power, a notion that goes a long way towards accounting for our preoccupation with the personality of presidents. Unfortunately, these issues are not thoroughly investigated in *American Politicians.*

Kismaric never actually provides a definition of "politician," leaving readers to presume that all of the people whose pictures are included should be so considered. Thus, as no viewer will dispute, Abraham Lincoln, Calvin Coolidge and Bill Clinton are politicians, as are many other presidents. So too are Adlai Stevenson, Joseph McCarthy and Fiorello La Guardia, but then so are John Brown, Marcus Garvey, Abbie Hoffman and others for whom an argument might need to be made. This is not to say that Brown, Garvey and Hoffman are *not* politicians, only that the author

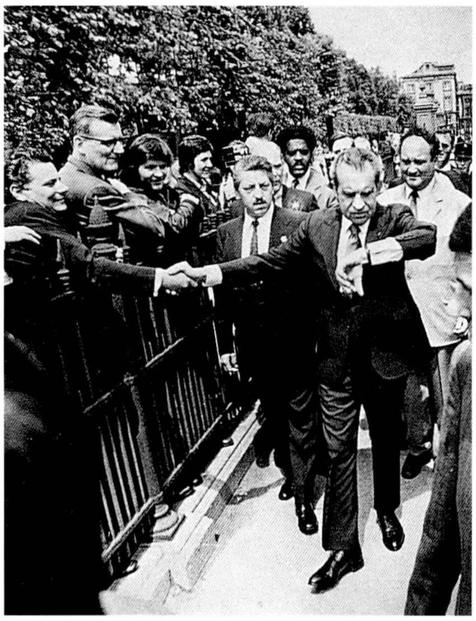

Horst Faas, *President Nixon in Belgium, 26 June 1974.* From *American Politicians.*

neglects to make a persuasive argument for their inclusion.

In avoiding a definition of who and what is a politician, she also avoids defining "politics," again assuming a self-evident definition. Politics, for Kismaric, is *electoral* politics, but there are many other kinds. A politics of representation, for example, presumes that no form of depiction—verbal, visual or any other—is innocent of the motivations of those who create, disseminate or consume it. In this view, photography is inextricable from any process into which it is inserted, an awareness that largely is missing from *American Politicians.* When Kismaric discusses instances in which photography has been used to create or alter public impressions of a politician, her analysis lacks depth. Noting Theodore Roosevelt's attention to reporters, photographers and publicity of all kinds, she speaks of a picture of Roosevelt operating a steam shovel during the construction of the Panama Canal, yet merely comments that it "provides a fine example of how his image was projected." This not only says nothing about what *kind* of image he sought to project, but, in a more crucial omission, why he sought to project it, or why the photographer participated in this celebration of archetypally American he-man bravado. It ignores the historical circumstances that surround the making of the photograph, specifically the quest for world dominance that motivated the building of the canal.

Rather than consider the importance of historical circumstances, *American Politicians* dwells on aspects of formalism. The scheme by which the photographs and accompanying text are organized is the strictly formal one of chronology, and the driving force of the chronology is technology: as time passes, photographic technology improves, and as technology improves, so does the ability of the photographer to represent the desired subject. The implication is that the photographs—or, more accurately, the forms taken by the photographs—change because the technology changes, and not because of any alterations in the practice of politics or in American society.

This way of looking at photographs may be irresponsible, and in this case is certainly regrettable, but it is by no means new. John Szarkowski, for whom Kismaric once worked at the Museum of Modern Art, spent most of his curatorial career attempting to demonstrate that all photographs, from the highest of high art to the lowest of snapshots, shared a common bond: the aesthetic of the photographic. He argued his point, as does Kismaric, by downplaying the historical situation connected with any given photograph and the uses to which it was put, and by paying attention to its formal properties. One of the more extreme products of this procedure is probably the most direct precedent for *American Politicians.* In *From the Picture Press* (Museum of Modern Art, 1973), Szarkowski presented photographs from the files of the *New York Daily News* without any information other than the photographer's name, the picture agency and the date. Details about subject matter and other such trivialities were relegated to an appendix. Szarkowski's stated intention was to show that "the formal and iconographic character of news photographs has made a significant contribution to the development of the modern visual vocabulary." In other words, the accidents of framing, lighting, stop-action and other techniques that were abundantly present in news photographs made them look just like the pictures of an entire generation of self-conscious art photographers who had made such accidents the basis of their aesthetic.

The heroes of that generation of photography—Robert Frank the progenitor, Garry Winogrand and Lee Friedlander the anointed successors—are absent from Szarkowski's book, but they are very much present in *American Politicians.* Each is given a small block of pictures, thus extending Szarkowski's premise in *From the Picture Press* one step forward. Still, in other respects, this book represents a retrograde view of photography. As one of the few photography publications to come out of the Museum of Modern Art since Szarkowski's retirement, *American Politicians* indicates that thinking in that quarter has changed very little.

Triumph of the Fact-Checker
In **see** 1:1, mention was made of *Triumph of the Will* in Mark Alice Durant's review of *Radiant Identities.* The actual title of the Leni Riefenstahl film in question is *Olympia.*

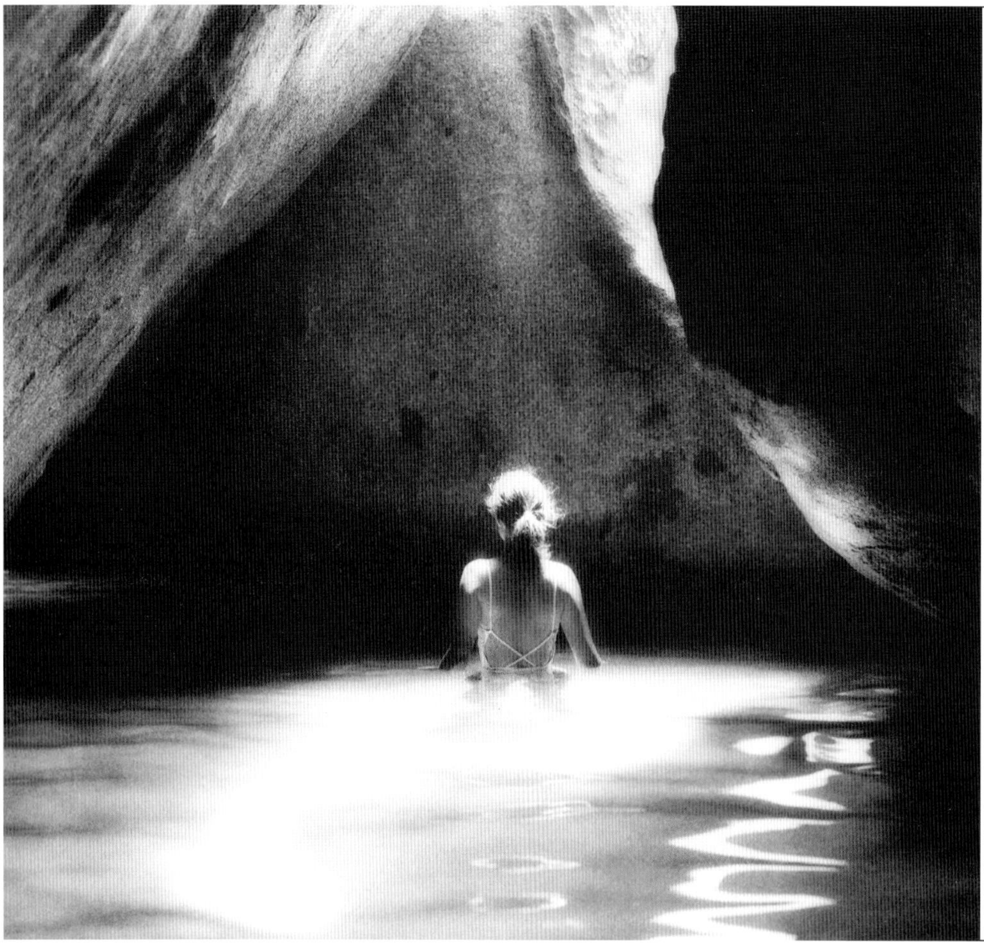

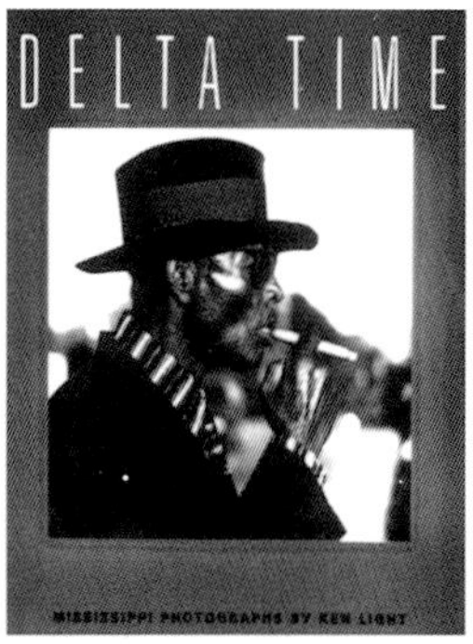

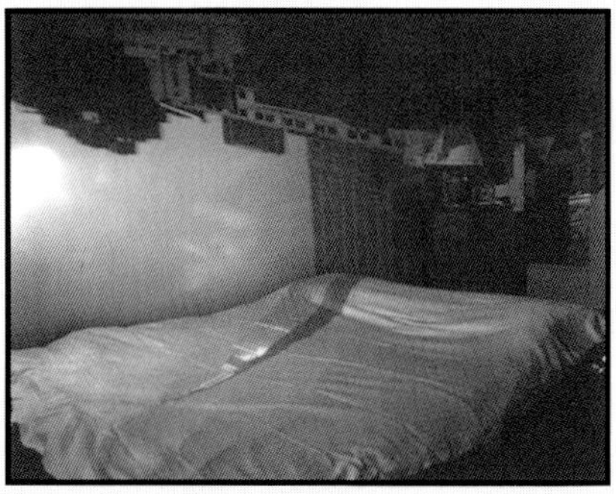

Camera Obscura Image of the Empire State Building in Bedroom by Abelardo Morell. © 1994. Courtesy of Bonni Benrubi Gallery, New York, N.Y.

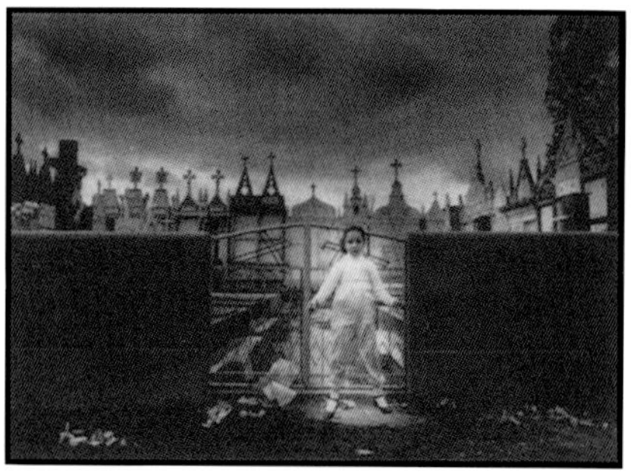

El Alma Dormida (The Sleeping Soul), Saavedra, Galicia, 1981.

SOUND AND VISION

BIG IDEAS, IMAGES AND DISTORTED FACTS

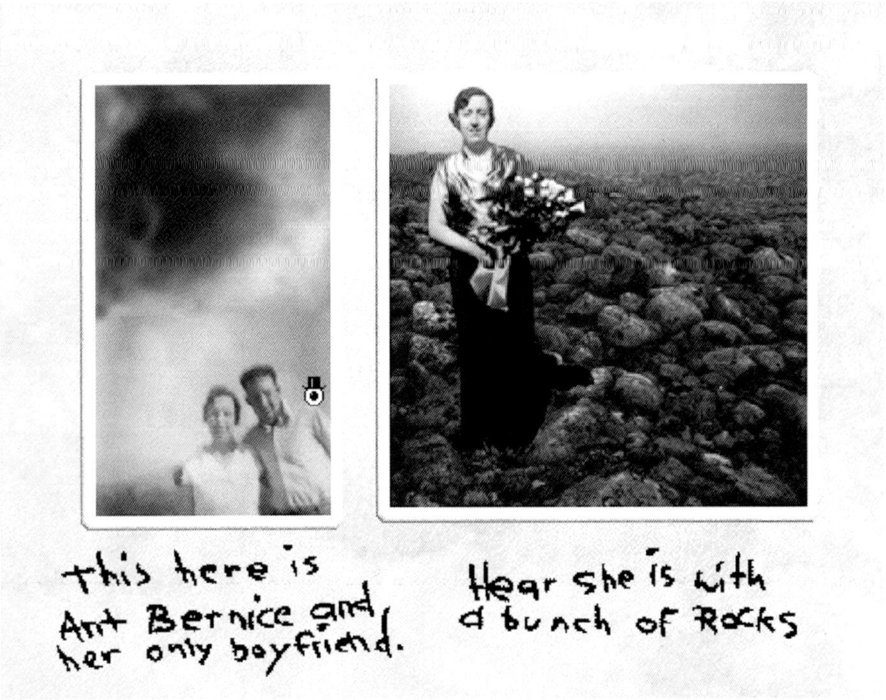

A page from Benny the Bump's scrapbook. From The Residents Freak Show.

Bob Dylan: Highway 61 Interactive
Graphix Zone, 1995

The Residents Freak Show
Voyager, 1994

Review by Michael Read

As the shimmering, guiding principle of Cyberspace, interactivity is touted as a ticket to the final frontier. The question, however, remains: are we truly interacting with our computers, or merely interfacing? Time for a virtual reality check. All evidence indicates that our relationship with the machines still is based on the classic master-servant paradigm. The notion that we soon will be *interacting* with computers, rather than merely telling them what to do, has thus far proven to be an elusive holy grail. The bottom line: no matter how much Intel is inside, our computers won't do squat unless we switch them on first.

As luck would have it, most of them already are switched on. *We've been promised interactivity, dammit!* The entertainment industry, perhaps desperate to distract us from the fact that they still haven't produced credible virtual reality goggles, has stepped forward to keep us occupied with meaningful new technologies that are ever more compatible with human reason. Unfortunately, all they've come up with are a bunch of CD-ROMs.

A typical CD-ROM title—whether it's *Stephen Jay Gould: On Evolution* or *Macbeth Karaoke* or *Death Cycles from Hell*—offers a formidable menu of words, images and sounds for sampling. But sadly, one can only get out of this virtual box of chocolates what someone else has put into it (namely, the programmers). And yes, it's true: those shiny little discs can hold only a finite number of 1s and 0s. As with everything else in life, in the end our choices are limited. So that's the way it is—in this brave new world of CD-ROM media, freedom of choice is peddled off as interactivity.

That said, once we let go of the notion that interactivity is our birthright, CD-ROM technology can be appreciated on its own terms. Our new ability to bake image, text, sound and motion in one virtual pie surely makes for a tastier, if not interactive, interaction. Two recent titles from the music industry—the spawning ground of popular digital culture—display considerable flair and promise for the future (forced optimism notwithstanding). At the very least, *Bob Dylan: Highway 61 Interactive* and *The Residents Freak Show* are redeemed by sheer entertainment value alone.

Those shiny little discs can hold only a finite number of 1s and 0s. As with everything else in life, in the end our choices are limited.

The Dylan disc promises "an interactive experience in the virtual world of legendary singer, songwriter, poet & culture shaker Bob Dylan." According to the instruction manual, the primary interface, an image collage composed of flotsam and jetsam from Dylan's thirty-year career, "is full of hot objects including morphs (things that change shape into other things), animations, and sound recordings. Many of the pieces will take you to 3-D environments that you can explore for hours." These "hot objects"—ticket stubs, maps, a typewriter, various musical instruments, a television set, an hourglass, a cup of coffee—turn out to be merely cool. They are, in essence, simply buttons, not unlike the one that Koko the trained gorilla pressed when she wanted another banana. For instance, click on the hourglass and a sound byte from—*surprise, surprise*—"The Times They Are A-Changin'" emanates from your computer. It doesn't take long for this inane cause-and-effect dynamic to get predictable and even tedious; presumably, even gorillas grow weary of bananas.

More interesting are the navigable 3-D environments that *Highway 61 Interactive* creates, among them New York Columbia Studios in 1965, two coffee houses where Dylan performed in the early stages of his career, and, best of all, the streets of Greenwich Village circa 1962. Accessed by clicking the mouse on an image of the famous arch at Washington Square, the Village environment has an appealing, nostalgic aura. By following the mouse (yes, it's come to following mice), it is possible to meander down streets and alleys, to read newspapers from a newsstand, pop into cafés and record stores, and even sit in on a spirited rehearsal by a gospel choir in a storefront church.

Virtual tourism can be entertaining, but the subject at hand here is supposed to be Bob Dylan. Instead of seeking to illuminate the mind of the man who invited us to "see the primitive wallflower freeze when the jelly-faced women all sneezed," this disc trivializes Dylan's singular achievement. What, for instance, is gained by including Pearl Jam singer Eddie Vedder's vacuous reflections on Dylan's career? In the end, *Highway 61 Interactive* turns out to be little more than a glorified press release for Dylan's induction into the Rock and Roll Hall of Fame.

As is often the story in Medialand, a worthy idea has been corrupted by cynical, dollars-driven market positioning. The disc's publisher, Graphix Zone, even has the audacity to assert that "The demographics of Bob Dylan fans match those of PC users." As Dylan sang in *Idiot Wind,* "Their minds are filled with big ideas, images and distorted facts."

The jelly-faced women of Dylan's imagination would be right at home in *The Residents Freak Show,* a brilliant CD-ROM published by Voyager. Primarily known as the tuxedo-clad dancing eyeballs from their album covers, The Residents have been influencing trends in popular culture since 1970. That was the year the music/performance/media troupe from San Mateo, California released their first single, "Santa Dog," and helped set the stage for digital sampling by substituting a multi-track recorder for live musical instruments. Their 1976 video *The Third Reich and Roll* is noted as a pioneering step in the development of the music video form. Subsequent projects, such as the ambitious 1982 traveling review *Mole Show,* continued to blaze new paths for musical theatre and multimedia performance. With *Freak Show,* the dancing eyeballs continue to display their caustic wit and knack for innovation. In the process, they have helped to create a promising new form for digital multimedia: the fictional narrative as a navigable space.

Freak Show primarily is a collection of interconnected stories about the down-and-out inhabitants of a fantastic circus sideshow. Upon entering this bizarre big top, your chain-smoking, gin-guzzling host, Tex the Barker, introduces freaks with names like Wanda the Worm Woman, Jelly Jack the Boneless Boy and Bouncing Benny the Bump. After a series of truly bizarre sideshow spectacles, the real fun begins as you sneak backstage, heedless of the "No Trespassing" signs, to the seedy trailer park that the performers call home.

Once there, you are free to exercise your innate voyeuristic tendencies without consequence. Snoop through The Bump's photo album. Watch Wanda the Worm Woman floss her teeth after snacking on a dish of Night Crawlers. Pour a few drinks for Tex as he ruminates about his lost innocence. Each character has his or her own twisted story to be discovered as you navigate through their interior lives. For instance: Mickey the Mumbling Midget is not really an inarticulate dwarf, but in actuality is a shaved baboon who is prisoner to his forbidden desire for a beautiful collie.

Needless to say, spending a few hours in The Residents' alternate universe can be a disturbing, but thoroughly captivating, experience. The sounds and images within create a rich, multifaceted narrative that transcends the simplistic linear storytelling structures to which we have become accustomed. Here's the new world of storytelling, where images and sounds dislodge dialogue and description as the rudimentary building blocks of narrative. With *Freak Show,* The Residents have suggested the maturing of a new audiovisual, literary form through which users can manipulate the intricacies of plot in accordance with their own whimsy.

If *Highway 61* and *Freak Show* sound interactive, they are—but only as much as thumbing through a magazine or channel surfing. It's still just a walk from point A to point B (with short detours to points Q, M and P along the way). If you keep your eyes open and your expectations in check, this walk through unknown territories may prove to be worthwhile after all.

CONTRIBUTORS

KIKU ADATTO has taught American culture and photography at Harvard University and is the author of *Picture Perfect: The Art and Artifice of Public Image Making* (Basic Books, 1993). Her column, "Public Images," debuts in this issue and will appear regularly in see.

DAVID BRESKIN is a San Francisco-based poet with poems forthcoming in *Poetry East, Alaska Quarterly Review* and *The Amicus Journal.* His writing also has appeared in *The New Yorker, The Paris Review* and *New American Writing.*

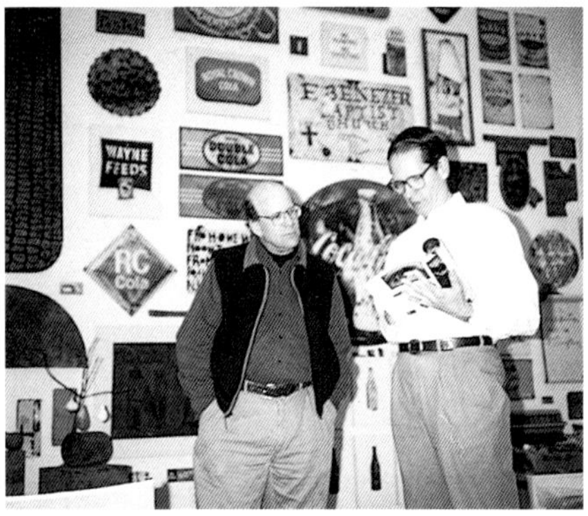

David Levinthal and William Christenberry
Photo by Merry Foresta.

WILLIAM CHRISTENBERRY is a sculptor and photographer living in Washington, D.C., where he teaches at The Corcoran School of Art. Born in Hale County, Alabama, he has made the South and its heritage the focus of his work for more than twenty years, most notably in his elaborate *The Klan Room* tableaux.

JAMES CRUMP lives in Santa Fe. He has written for *The New Art Examiner* and *History of Photography.* His recent publications include *George Platt Lynes: Photographs From The Kinsey Institute* (Little, Brown, 1993) and *Harm's Way,* a book of photographs edited by Joel-Peter Witkin (Twin Palms, 1994).

MERRY FORESTA is Curator of Photography at the National Museum of American Art, Smithsonian Institution. She is the author of many articles and books on photography, including *Between Home and Heaven: Contemporary American Landscape Photography* (Smithsonian Institution, 1992).

RICK HOCK currently is Director of Creative Services at George Eastman House. He teaches Fine Art Photography at the Rochester Institute of Technology and is the recipient of two National Endowment for the Arts Photography fellowships. His "Open Space" project for see is an extension of his *Codex* series, which narrates history through collections of existing images.

Inscrutable Objects was an exhibition organized by Andy Grundberg and presented at the Ansel Adams Center for Photography, San Francisco, in March 1995. Among its artists: JO ANN CALLIS lives in Los Angeles and has taught photography for twenty years at the California Institute for the Arts and UCLA. She has exhibited throughout America and in Japan. JEANNE DUNNING lives and teaches in Chicago. Her ambiguous, body-centered photographs have been widely exhibited. She is represented by Feature Gallery of New York. ANN MANDELBAUM teaches at Pratt Institute in New York. Her solarized and rephotographed images of body parts and small objects are reproduced in the book *Ann Mandelbaum* (Edition Stennle, 1994). SUZANNE OPTON was born in Portland and studied philosophy at Smith College. She lives in New York and has taught photography at Pratt and at the School of Visual Arts. GAY OUTLAW is a photographer and sculptor who shows at Photos Gallery in San Francisco. ELLIOT SCHWARTZ lives in New York, where his work has been shown at the International Center of Photography and Jayne Baum Gallery. He studied photography at Yale University, where he developed his fascination with the functional mystery of industrial and ethnographic objects. KENNETH SHORR is a photographer and scavenger who finds his sculptural materials preserved in the desert near his home in Tucson, Arizona. He also is a performance artist. JANICE TANNIN now lives in New York City after a long stint in Oakland. She received a Murphy Fellowship from the San Francisco Foundation while studying for her MFA at Mills College. Her work has been shown at the Rena Bransten Gallery in San Francisco.

DAVID LEVINTHAL has been making images that recapitulate cultural and historical iconography for more than twenty years. In the *Mein Kampf* series, first shown at Janet Borden Inc. in New York, he returns to the period of his first book, *Hitler Moves East,* written with Gary Trudeau. Other Levinthal books include *Desire* (The Friends of Photography, 1993).

MICHAEL LIGHT is a photographer and creator of sculptural installations that address the American environment. *Blue Fall* originated as a large floor installation that invited viewers to look down, much like passengers on an airplane. Light's toned aerial photographs are made from his window seat on various commercial airline flights across America. A recent graduate of the MFA program at the San Francisco Art Institute, Light's first book is *Ranch* (Twelvetrees Press/Twin Palms Publishing, 1993).

MARTHA MADIGAN lives in Philadelphia and chairs the Department of Photography at Tyler School of Art/Temple University. Madigan has worked with large-scale solar photograms for more than twenty years. Madigan's work in this issue is from her series *Second Nature.* Madigan is represented by Michael Rosenfeld Gallery, New York.

DAN MEINWALD is completing a Ph.D. in art history at the University of California, Santa Barbara. He has been writing about photography since 1977 in publications such as *AfterImage* and *Exposure.*

RENNY PRITIKIN is the Artistic Director of the Center for the Arts at Yerba Buena Gardens, San Francisco, and a poet, writer and curator. His essay originated as a gallery talk for the *Snapshots* series at the Ansel Adams Center for Photography.

C.P. ROSENTHAL's fourth novel, *Elena of the Stars,* will be published this fall by St. Martin's Press. "Rise and Fall of the New West" is part of a forthcoming volume of related short stories titled *Zen Cowboy*. Rosenthal lives in Topanga Canyon, California and teaches at Loyola Marymount University in Los Angeles.

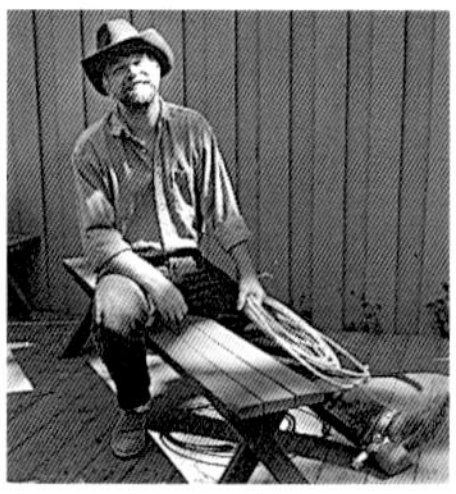

C.P. Rosenthal
Photo by Bill Freimuth.

FAZAL SHEIKH studied with Emmet Gowin at Princeton University and received the 1995 Ferguson and 1995 Ruttenberg Foundation grants from The Friends of Photography. He is the first photographer to win both awards in the same year. Sheikh received a 1994 Infinity Award from the International Center of Photography, and a fellowship from the National Endowment for the Arts. His work in this issue recently was shown at the Pace/MacGill Gallery in New York.

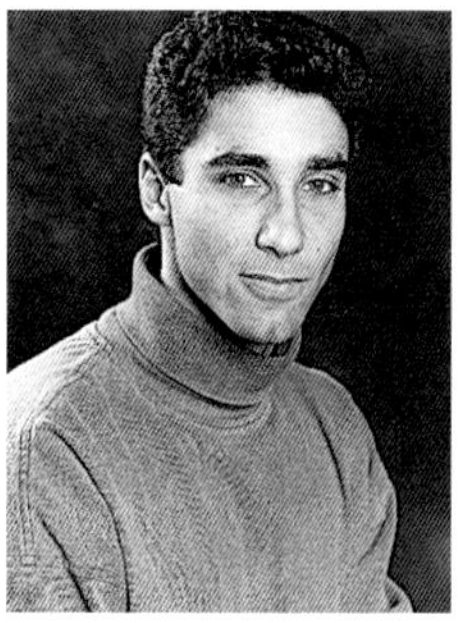

Fazal Sheikh
Photo by Denise Applewhite.

VALERIE SOE is a teacher, writer and filmmaker living in San Francisco, and a founding member of X-Factor. Her acclaimed film and video pieces include *Black Sheep* and *Picturing Oriental Girls: A (Re)Educational Videotape.*

CARLA WILLIAMS lives and works in Los Angeles.

STATE OF THE

ART

O.J. DISORDER

BY ANDY GRUNDBERG

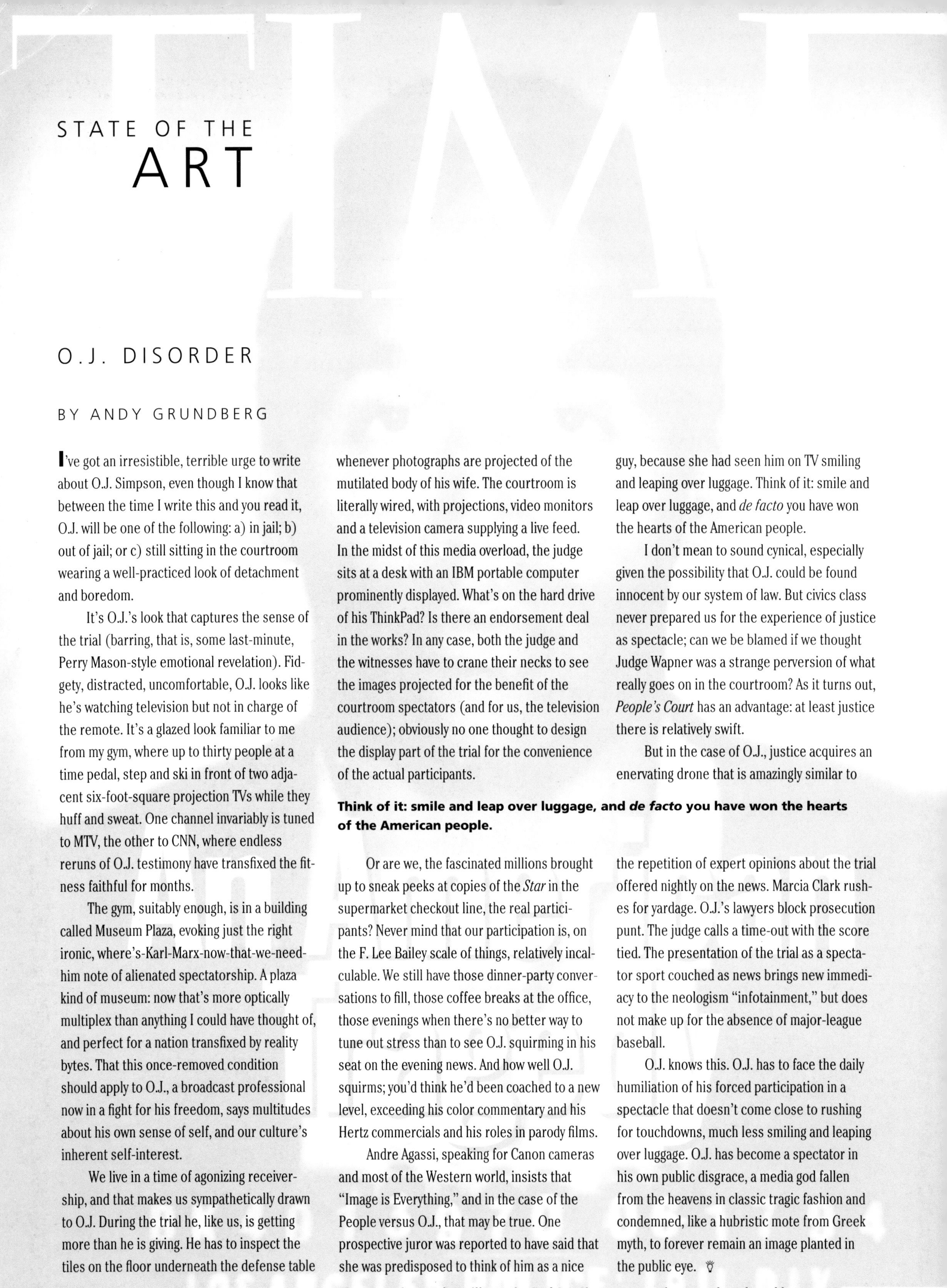

I've got an irresistible, terrible urge to write about O.J. Simpson, even though I know that between the time I write this and you read it, O.J. will be one of the following: a) in jail; b) out of jail; or c) still sitting in the courtroom wearing a well-practiced look of detachment and boredom.

It's O.J.'s look that captures the sense of the trial (barring, that is, some last-minute, Perry Mason-style emotional revelation). Fidgety, distracted, uncomfortable, O.J. looks like he's watching television but not in charge of the remote. It's a glazed look familiar to me from my gym, where up to thirty people at a time pedal, step and ski in front of two adjacent six-foot-square projection TVs while they huff and sweat. One channel invariably is tuned to MTV, the other to CNN, where endless reruns of O.J. testimony have transfixed the fitness faithful for months.

The gym, suitably enough, is in a building called Museum Plaza, evoking just the right ironic, where's-Karl-Marx-now-that-we-need-him note of alienated spectatorship. A plaza kind of museum: now that's more optically multiplex than anything I could have thought of, and perfect for a nation transfixed by reality bytes. That this once-removed condition should apply to O.J., a broadcast professional now in a fight for his freedom, says multitudes about his own sense of self, and our culture's inherent self-interest.

We live in a time of agonizing receivership, and that makes us sympathetically drawn to O.J. During the trial he, like us, is getting more than he is giving. He has to inspect the tiles on the floor underneath the defense table whenever photographs are projected of the mutilated body of his wife. The courtroom is literally wired, with projections, video monitors and a television camera supplying a live feed. In the midst of this media overload, the judge sits at a desk with an IBM portable computer prominently displayed. What's on the hard drive of his ThinkPad? Is there an endorsement deal in the works? In any case, both the judge and the witnesses have to crane their necks to see the images projected for the benefit of the courtroom spectators (and for us, the television audience); obviously no one thought to design the display part of the trial for the convenience of the actual participants.

Think of it: smile and leap over luggage, and *de facto* you have won the hearts of the American people.

Or are we, the fascinated millions brought up to sneak peeks at copies of the *Star* in the supermarket checkout line, the real participants? Never mind that our participation is, on the F. Lee Bailey scale of things, relatively incalculable. We still have those dinner-party conversations to fill, those coffee breaks at the office, those evenings when there's no better way to tune out stress than to see O.J. squirming in his seat on the evening news. And how well O.J. squirms; you'd think he'd been coached to a new level, exceeding his color commentary and his Hertz commercials and his roles in parody films.

Andre Agassi, speaking for Canon cameras and most of the Western world, insists that "Image is Everything," and in the case of the People versus O.J., that may be true. One prospective juror was reported to have said that she was predisposed to think of him as a nice guy, because she had seen him on TV smiling and leaping over luggage. Think of it: smile and leap over luggage, and *de facto* you have won the hearts of the American people.

I don't mean to sound cynical, especially given the possibility that O.J. could be found innocent by our system of law. But civics class never prepared us for the experience of justice as spectacle; can we be blamed if we thought Judge Wapner was a strange perversion of what really goes on in the courtroom? As it turns out, *People's Court* has an advantage: at least justice there is relatively swift.

But in the case of O.J., justice acquires an enervating drone that is amazingly similar to the repetition of expert opinions about the trial offered nightly on the news. Marcia Clark rushes for yardage. O.J.'s lawyers block prosecution punt. The judge calls a time-out with the score tied. The presentation of the trial as a spectator sport couched as news brings new immediacy to the neologism "infotainment," but does not make up for the absence of major-league baseball.

O.J. knows this. O.J. has to face the daily humiliation of his forced participation in a spectacle that doesn't come close to rushing for touchdowns, much less smiling and leaping over luggage. O.J. has become a spectator in his own public disgrace, a media god fallen from the heavens in classic tragic fashion and condemned, like a hubristic mote from Greek myth, to forever remain an image planted in the public eye.

Time **magazine's "photo-illustration" of O.J. Simpson, a routine mug shot altered by computer by Matt Mahurin. From the start, O.J. has been the prisoner of a media spectacle.**